I0788019

Bewitched, Bothered and Bipolar

Judy Lanteigne

Published by New Generation Publishing in 2021

Copyright © Judy Lanteigne 2021

First Edition

The author asserts the moral right under the Copyright, Designs and Patents Act 1988 to be identified as the author of this work.

All Rights reserved. No part of this publication may be reproduced, stored in a retrieval system or transmitted, in any form or by any means without the prior consent of the author, nor be otherwise circulated in any form of binding or cover other than that which it is published and without a similar condition being imposed on the subsequent purchaser.

ISBN
Paperback   978-1-80369-053-7
Hardback   978-1-80369-054-4

Cover design and book sketches by Judy Lanteigne.

www.newgeneration-publishing.com

New Generation Publishing

To Bridget,

who always kept me in my airport

Contents

Introduction

Our language is decidedly sparse when it comes to expressing our emotions, so it's a complex task to describe in words the extremes of emotions you encounter when you sink to the depths of depression as well as to the euphoric heights bipolar conversely affords you. As you then feel a desperate need to share the revelations of your journey with others, the way left to you is through creativity, be it writing, poetry or painting.

The prescribed lock-down during the time of the Covid pandemic of 2020/21 was the perfect time for me to start writing my book about bipolar disorder and the way it's affected my life. Although I have lived with the disorder, I'm not a trained expert on the subject so I've looked for confirmation of my views from various medical specialists. Notwithstanding, the views I have expressed on the subject are my own.

I have heard it suggested that creativity comes from the yearning to live on beyond one's inevitable death. What you create – in your struggle for immortality, thereafter becomes your legacy. Stanley Kunitz, an American poet Laureate wrote that 'the poet writes his poems out of his rage.' A rage he explains, about the greatest injustice of all – death. Dylan Thomas wrote, 'Do not go gentle into that good night. Rage, rage against the dying of the light.'

Another possibility is that we create to overcompensate for our inadequacies, as with Beethoven who was deaf and Byron who was born with a club foot, or even Keats whose family suffered from TB which eventually killed him too.

How do we account for Hemingway whose writing earned the admiration of the world but who spent much of his life revelling in brutal bullfights in Spain as well as being a big game hunter in Africa and deep sea fishing off the American east coast; enacting brutal killings on a worldwide scale. This being apart from his job as a war correspondent, opportunistically keeping many events to himself as material for his books. His father killed himself, his three brothers died and eventually he took the gun to himself. Was he compensating for his debilitating depressions and larger than life personality, or did he suffer from bipolar disorder and was writing the result of his desperate yearning for a creative outlet?

Is creativity a neurosis; is talent a disease? According to Sigmund Freud, who founded the discipline of psychoanalysis; neurosis is a coping strategy caused by unsuccessfully repressed emotions from past experiences. Carl Gustav Jung, his former student, who founded analytical psychology, believed that neurosis was a clash of conscious and unconscious events in the mind.

Do we use creativity to make sense of our existence? Descartes existentially stated 'Cogito ergo sum' - I think, therefore I am, but we are so much more than mere thinkers, we experience a multitude of emotions throughout our lives which we need to come to terms with and shape into recognisable patterns and meanings.

A definition of creativity online; suggests it is the act of turning new and imaginative ideas into reality. It is characterised by the ability to perceive the world in new ways, to find hidden patterns, to make connections between seemingly unrelated phenomena, and to generate solutions.

According to the author, Thomas Disch, 'Creativeness is the ability to see relationships where none exist.' Rollo May, in his book *The Courage to Create* states, 'Creativity requires passion and commitment. It brings to our awareness what was previously hidden and points to new life. The experience is one of heightened consciousness: ecstasy.'

Bipolar disorder frequently leads you on a capricious journey of unique emotions; whether to experience unfathomable deep waters or be wafted into an ecstatic infinity. Creativity can sometimes be the only way to assimilate such shattering passions, and attempt to find a satisfying way to express them. Or as James Joyce appositely put it, 'Forge in the smithy of their soul!'

Judy Lanteigne

Bewitched Bothered & Bipolar

Chapter 1

ELEMENTALS

It would be reasonable to question how it is possible for a person to harbour a capricious mental disorder and be unaware of it until late in their life. And yet this was the case for me with this little understood condition, as I only fully accepted I was bipolar as I was approaching my seventieth birthday.

Some years previously, I had finally divorced my husband, Mike, and was on my own, bringing up my two sons. I was not awarded enough in maintenance payments from Mike to avoid the need to find full-time work to support us, so I had managed to find a full-time job in London, working initially in the training department of Visnews, a company formed for television news broadcasts by the BBC, CBC, NZBC, ABC and Reuters. For a time I was their PR assistant, ensuring the media and personnel stationed around the globe had access to information about the world of TV news.

There I met Martin, a Canadian, who, as a bureau chief in Jerusalem, had been recalled to London as a political move and whose wife refused to visit the UK after a year she'd previously spent there. Subsequently, he was to return alone and seemed keen to make a beeline for me, making it difficult for me to get in or out of the building without encountering him. I had only recently recovered from an abortive affair with another married man, so initially I resisted his advances, but he fitted my idealised picture of a man in many ways and eventually wore me down. He later resigned from Visnews and left for Canada and a job as a TV producer for the CBC network to Brian Mulroney, the prime minister. Owing to my relationship with my father, I had already been programmed to long for men who largely remained distant from me, only to return for short, exciting visits, and so Martin and I began a long-distance affair.

In the spring of 1996, Martin invited me to stay with him in the Maritimes, the coastal provinces in the east of Canada that include New Brunswick and the islands of Nova Scotia and Prince Edward. He was living in a flat downtown in Fredericton and across from the flat were some of the most beautifully carved wooden houses that looked as though they'd be more at home on a film set, as well as a large spreading tree that slowly came back to life day by day as its leaves slowly unfurled.

As a consequence of that visit's impact on me, I vowed to return to find somewhere I could paint in such unspoilt and inspirational surroundings. Being of a restless nature, I was to commute regularly to Canada for many years after that to paint, and bought two different houses there in the process.

I was desperately keen to work on large paintings that I hoped might communicate to others what I felt I had learned from a series of spiritual books that I believed had helped me become more proactive and positive about my life – and which I felt provided a more sustainable and compassionate way to live. I didn't have the room in my cottage for such an activity, but it was something that seemed imperative at the time. I became a woman on a mission.

My usual Canada commute was generally sometime around mid-May. In that way I had the best of both worlds with the seasons, since every year I could watch the spring flowers bloom, trees blossom and turn the very air viridescent with burgeoning green leaves in the UK, then I could watch the exciting spring spectacle begin all over again when I reached the Maritimes.

However, just when you think that your life has reached a comfortable plateau, you can guarantee that the gods will be busy devising a few more challenges for you. So it was to be for me in the summer of 2004. I had only been back in Canada for a while and had settled back into life there again when I had a call to tell me my ex-husband, Mike, had been carried off to hospital by ambulance and there were serious fears for his life. I immediately felt the need to fly back to the UK and begged Air Canada for a compassion ticket so I could at least be there for my sons. Also, I had always harboured romantic ideas that when the time came to say a final goodbye, we would enjoy a brief moment of reunion and all would be forgiven – quite an absurd fantasy in the circumstances. When I arrived, I found my younger son Nicky waiting to take me to the hospital. The huge bulk in the bed that I looked down upon that day was Mike. He was already in a coma and he never woke again.

The following year, I received more disturbing news. Nicky was suffering from what had been diagnosed as inherited hypobipolar disorder and needed to be hospitalised immediately. It seemed likely that the stress he'd experienced after the death of his father had set the disorder in motion.

I was no stranger to mental illness. For years doctors had been prescribing lithium carbonate for me during periods of depression, and I remembered that when I had asked my doctor for a health report for an art therapy course I planned to attend, I found that bipolar disorder was included on my NHS records. I had demanded at the time that the doctor strike it off and replace it with reactive depression.

The thought of the hereditary aspect of Nicky's illness immediately threw me back into one of my self-disparaging, dark depressions. Had Nicky inherited his disorder from me? Had I somehow contributed to it? This led me to unravel my own journey with mental illness over a seventy-year period and forced me to finally start accepting the possibility that I had myself been struggling all my life with this disruptive disorder as well.

But what is bipolar? How could I have lived with it all my life and not known? What causes it? And how can we successfully treat it? I was determined to discover the answers and to find a way to deal with the disorder.

On top of this was another question. I had experienced plenty of 'lows' in my life, and had even attempted suicide at times, but I'd also had incredible 'highs'. And with those 'highs' had come the most intense and rewarding periods of creativity and enlightenment. Could there be a link between bipolar and creativity? And if so, would we want to cure bipolar even if we could?

After hearing the doctor's diagnosis of Nicky's illness, I didn't feel I could allow myself to go on enjoying my carefree life in the Maritimes. Nicky had worked so hard and been so ambitious, and now it seemed his life was in a destructive and earth-plunging nosedive. I felt I had to go back to the UK and try to prevent his situation becoming worse and ruining what should have been a glittering future for him. In the process, I was to explore my own relationship with bipolar, its causes and its current methods of treatment.

This is my story about how an often-misunderstood disability can disrupt a life. Of course, no one likes to be pigeon-holed with a medical pathology. However, surviving this particular disorder is a mental challenge in itself, as it is one that can remain undetected by others as well as by the individual who succumbs to it. Plus, no one yet seems to really understand it and why it hasn't been phased out of our genes throughout our aeons of history. It's only since the early 1970s that any standard diagnostic methods have even been recognised.

Bipolar remains one of the most misunderstood mental health conditions. If you imagine you have learned much about it from watching a certain actress cope with this condition on a TV series called *Homeland*, don't be fooled. This disorder is far more nuanced than could be presented in a TV programme by an actress.

It's true to say few people get through life unscathed and it can for some seem appallingly unfair; but faced with such an alarming array of nascent stumbling blocks, I somehow seem to have survived so far to tell my tale, although I'm still fully aware that life never tires of providing shocks and has scant disregard for age.

Initially it never occurred to me that my passion to create could have anything to do with any mental disorder. I was only aware that I was always happy to lose myself when I embarked on a creative project of any kind and found that the hours slipped by contentedly while I was thus immersed. Now that I have finally come to terms with bipolar, I realise that possibly much of my itinerant lifestyle and restlessness has been prompted by the condition and I am keen to explore the diverse aspects of it in this book while pleading for a better understanding of some of its more negative characteristics – especially considering its creative contribution to society.

Chapter 2

WHAT CAUSES BIPOLAR?

My birth in the spring of 1940 was one that was obviously abysmally timed, being at the start of World War II. But it allowed my family to make me the butt of a family joke as to how my birth had activated a world war. I always felt the need to instantly remind everyone that I had, in fact, been born six months after it broke out, and while I might share the same zodiac sign of Aries with *mein Fuhrer*, whose overweening ambitions started the last world war, there seem to be few other similarities – although my mother might at times have disagreed. But you know how literally children take things, never mind recalling my mother's insouciance at ascribing blame, which, added to her unflinching sarcasm, pretty much obliterating any hopes you might have of receiving your 'de jure' birthright - your intrinsic right to happiness.

Carl Jung is said to have stated: 'Nothing has a stronger influence psychologically on their environment and especially on their children than the unlived life of the parent.' Such could be said of my mother – but then life for women forced to cope alone after their men abandoned them and went off to war was hardly likely to be a satisfying or a fulfilled one.

My inability to build trustful relationships with my parents – a mother who could blow hot or cold and a father who apparently couldn't wait to abandon us after I was born – was unlikely to allow me to successfully invest in constructive relationships going forward.

At the age of thirty-five my father would certainly have been old enough to be exempt from war duty, but he happily signed up and was away for five years. These unfortunate circumstances, as well as the unsettled influence of World War II, were never going to give my formative years a healthy kick-start for my life ahead, even before I was aware I was going to be assailed by a capricious mental health hazard called bipolar disorder.

But is it the events and experiences of childhood that cause bipolar, or a genetic predisposition from before we were born? Given the diagnosis Nicky had received, I was keen to find out.

Genetic or Nurture?

The causes of bipolar are complex and not fully understood. A genetic factor has long been taken for granted, as Edward Bullmore, a world-wide expert in neuroscience asserts. He makes the point that depression is heritable, meaning that it runs in families doubling the risk three times if your parents are depressive and twofold for siblings. But he further points out that depression is not as heritable as perhaps schizophrenia or bipolar disorder.

In a study published in 2018 online, a large number of investigators did a DNA analysis from around 130,000 cases of depression and as many healthy individuals. As a result, for the first time, we are finding out some of the causes of depression.

However, in her book *The Successful Self*, psychologist Dorothy Rowe discusses the hereditary aspect of bipolar disorder in the chapter entitled 'Mania', where she suggests that calling something like manic depression a hereditary condition immediately exonerates the family of cruel behaviour towards a child who, in adulthood, could be seen to display obvious symptoms of the disorder. It also absolves them from any responsibility regarding the patient's outrageous behaviour.

However, she maintains that the psychiatric belief that manic depression is a genetic disease has allowed many extraverts to use the disorder as a defence mechanism from making an analytical journey inwards to attempt to unearth the source of whatever terror they are trying to evade.

She further talks about a book entitled *Images of Destruction* by David Wigoder. The book has an introduction by the eminent psychiatrist Anthony Storr, who in describing the book as the rambling autobiography of a manic depressive, calls it a 'foray forward and backward that alternately fascinates and bores.' It seems at the age of thirteen, Wigoder (a pseudonym) plunged into a foggy period during which he rarely left his bedroom, feeling disturbed by strange sensations when he was awake and finding familiar rooms strange to him. People's voices seemed to echo and even his own voice seemed to come from above him. By the age of forty, he recounts how he had ruined two promising careers, served a jail sentence after he'd attacked his wife with a garden tool and had subsequently become suicidal when he lost his profession and became isolated from his family and friends.

One morning, he woke up feeling fine. From then on, periods of depression alternated with periods of astonishing productivity and success – at school and then as an accountant. Further comments on the man's story, implies that anyone with psychiatric training would understand Wigoder's condition as manic depressive. He explains that the causes of the illness are not fully understood but are extensive. A genetic factor should be considered when it was revealed that his mother committed suicide when he was thirty-five years old.

However, Rowe points to the fact that anyone reading the book will soon appreciate that no one could have grown up in Wigoder's household and had the chance of becoming a healthy and secure adult. He frequently felt annihilated by his parents insensitive and unfeeling behaviour towards him, reducing him to suicidal feelings on a daily basis.

In attempting to make her point, Rowe explains how at the end of his book, Wigoder was eventually forced to accept his feelings of rage which is when he was able to make a change in his life and unravel his family's negative effect on his psyche.

So is bipolar the result of a faulty gene, or something to do with the circumstances of a child's upbringing? In other words, is it nature or nurture?

The 'good enough' mother

From studies on bipolar I found that, although it can be found clustered in families, other situations can also set it off. Take, for example, the concept of the vital mother–baby relationship. When it is born, a baby initially believes it is an extension of its mother's body. When it is time for it to accept its separateness, this can only succeed if it can start to see all other objects as 'not-me', so that there is now a 'me' and a 'not-me'.

This stage is only successful if the mother relationship has been, in the words of psychologist Donald Winnicott, 'good enough'. In this respect, therefore, the attachment of the mother is at first a delusion in the baby's mind and one that it has to be able to disallow in time. There then needs to be a substitution of the new self after the uncomfortable loss of the merged one. But the strength of the baby's ego will depend on the mother's support. If it does not receive this support, its sense of self is likely to be a feeble one going forward.

When a baby gets through the first stage and becomes aware it is not an extension of its mother's body and therefore has to separate, there comes the realisation that there are fearsome things 'out there'. At this point, when a child's fears overwhelm it and its carer is unable to break down its anxieties, it is unlikely to have the opportunity to learn how to deal with them. The child's fears will simply become overpowering and, as a coping skill, will split off into opposing polarities in an attempt to miss out the terrifying middle ground. This is the middle 'grey scale', which perhaps would have allowed them to find a balanced reality. Should that be denied them, it will then become a lifetime's challenge to effect any change.

When World War II broke out and my father went off to war, my mother was afraid to be on her own. She was then forced to give up following him around the country and, like many other families during the war, she moved in with various family members, living between her parents in Croydon and her sister-in-law's family in Guildford. For short periods of time my aunt's family became my extended family. Her daughter, who was eighteen months older than me, became my sister, while her older brothers become my future role models, one quiet and empathetic and the other a more radical figure. My Aunt Marion, my father's sister, was my godmother and was someone I found I could relate to. Despite having three children of her own, she had a way of making you feel you were the only one in the room with her. For the first time in my life, there was someone I could feel close to emotionally.

My father finally returned after the war when peace was at last declared and we moved back to the house my parents had built just before the war in Oxshott in Surrey. By then my younger sister had been born. She was five years younger than me and my father, who had originally made an enormous fuss of me and spoiled me rotten on all his short home leaves before abruptly disappearing again, totally ignored me to fuss over his new daughter. He made it clear that I was no longer of interest to him, and in response I found a pair of scissors and cut a huge swathe of hair on my head as it made me feel so ugly.

If Prince Harry feels his relationship with his father was a dysfunctional one, he is hardly alone. I have no memory of my father ever showing any affection towards me after he returned from the war, or indeed any interest in me. To me he was a cold, austere figure from whom there were never any signs of love or even approval, only a strange resentment when I started to stay out late with boyfriends in my late teens.

The body and the brain

In *The Inflamed Mind,* Professor Bullmore, while still clinging to the genetic explanation for bipolar, raises another possibility. He suggests depression could also be down to a gene called olfactomedin, better known for its effect on the gut system's response to bacteria. This is certainly a finding I can not only vouch for but directly relate to, since every emotional upset I encounter immediately reflects on my digestive system, resulting in my finding myself unable to function on many a morning after any emotional upheaval on the previous day. It can feel especially dispiriting when your energy levels are so low that you are unable to activate yourself. I can also remember my godmother, who frequently suffered with bilious attacks, often taking to her bed during upsets of this sort.

Many patients still have problems with their struggle to access joined-up medical treatment across the fatal flaw of Cartesian philosophy. It seems that Rene Descartes' analysis that the brain is a separate entity to the body is still instilled in many medical students. The consequence is that when it comes to finding a clinical service in the NHS for someone with psychosis or depression it is very difficult to find a practitioner who will treat the condition in a holistic way.

The subject came to the fore for me when I had an appointment with an oncology physician at a hospital and I pointed out that my stomach problems were more likely to be caused by my bipolar disorder than down to cancer. He appeared to be surprised, saying, 'How on earth did you know that?' I was surprised at his assumption that I must be stupid enough not to have made that connection.

Professor Bullmore asserts in his book that it's now perfectly clear that the mind and body are closely linked concluding that bodily inflamation can be seen to link across the blood brain barriers, causing inflamed brain cells and their networks. Social stress can cause bodily inflamation and this in turn would obviously effect mood and behaviour and be a risk for depression

So could bipolar originate in the gut?

We should try to remember that when we are babies the gut and the brain are minutely connected: we feel happy when we have had a feed and distinctly grizzly when we need to be winded. So even though this obviously becomes more refined with age, we are still irritable and disgruntled when our gut is out of sorts and its connection to the brain can cause severe feelings of hopelessness and depression, which can even show up in brain scans.

In her book *Gut,* the inside story of our body's most under-rated organ, Giulia Enders says, 'that an unhappy gut can be the cause of an unhappy mind.' She goes on to explain that it could be simply due to an undetected food intolerance – and the stomach has a right to be unhappy in such a circumstance. We should not therefore always blame depression on the brain – we are far more complicated than that.

During a recent tv programme titled *How Healthy is Your Gut* which attempted to explain why the gut is so important to a person's overall wellbeing, it was stated that the nation's digestion problems, thought to be due to stresses of life and poor diet, was an enormous financial burden on the NHS every year.

Enders goes on to point out that recent gut research has shown that we are much more than 'grey matter', and that recent research has shown that human self-awareness originates in the insular cortex.

The insular cortex plays a role in a variety of homeostatic functions related to basic survival needs, such as taste, visceral sensation and autonomic control. Enders likens each piece of information to a pixel pointing out that 'the insular cortex organises these pixels to form an overall image which represents a map of our feelings.'

Bullmore also acknowledges that the medical profession has been slow to acknowledge the necessity of integrating physical and mental health, not because doctors are heartless or incompetent, but because, 'The eye has a Cartesian blind spot, blinding us to our blindness - and something that's hiding in plain sight.' He describes it as, 'being unable to see something and not being able to see that we can't see.'

I have never personally been able to trace any genetic link to bipolar disorder in my own family background, as depression or a diagnosis of melancholia appear to have been the prevalent mental problems coming down the line. It was something my maternal grandmother and her eldest daughter, my mother's sister, suffered from. My mother's grandmother had died in an asylum, something my mother obviously found hard to acknowledge – presumably because she feared it might be genetic.

Indeed, the question then arises: if it is nurture instead of nature that is responsible for bipolar disorder, could I still have passed it down to my own sons?

My pregnancies as well as their childhoods were certainly disrupted by their father's volatile rages, which could be triggered by any number of things and erupt unpredictably, as well as his physical violence towards me when he felt the need to lash out – something he never made any attempt to hide from them. Mike was not only tall and proportionately large but was also an extremely overbearing man in his manner, especially when angry. His behaviour certainly generated more deeply depressive mood swings in me, no doubt adding to the disorder I already suffered from and leaving two sensitive and overly intelligent young boys unsettled and insecure. Added to this were the times when I felt compelled to leave my home with them and also, at times, without them, making them unsure as to when I might return.

Nicky's diagnosis had been termed as inherited hypomanic bipolar disorder. He was hearing voices and seeing people who were not there, including myself and his father. I learned more about the impacts on childhood from a radio interview on *The Life Scientific* programme entitled 'Why madness is in the world and not in us'. Interviewee Richard Bentall, a psychologist, maintains that people suffer from psychosis as adults after having suffered with shocks during their childhood. My boys had a father who regularly lost his temper, and shouted, bullied and lashed out at their mother, who was herself a bipolar disorder sufferer. What could be more shocking for a young sensitive child? My elder son, Leon, later told me, 'It was like growing up in a war zone!'

Trauma can have a dramatic effect on health via the cells of the body, which are, of course, in every part of our body. This is sometimes called cellular memory and even if you think you have forgotten something, your body hasn't. The more traumatic the event, the more dramatic the effect will be that is left behind, as cells impact everything, from the expression of our genes to the physical functioning of the body and actions, thoughts and emotions. The earlier these dramatic experiences take place, the more they affect us and form the basis for our cell's memories in the body.

Perhaps if I'd realised I was suffering from bipolar disorder, things might well have been different. Reaching adulthood with undiagnosed bipolar can be highly dangerous, as suicide is unfortunately a fundamental and sometimes unavoidable consequence of this type of mental illness, although apparently more common in men than in women and especially, I understand, in those aged over forty-five and living alone. There was certainly depression in my family, but no one until me had apparently suffered with what was still generally called manic depression at the time.

It's possible that growing up during a world war with an inability to find any common bond with my mother, my main caregiver, or my father, who was away during my formative years, means that it was brought on by environmental factors – nurture rather than nature. There is also the possibility that it was intrauterine, considering that war had been declared during my mother's pregnancy and she was presumably aware that her husband was about to abandon her.

In one sense, every depression is a biological issue because our neural transmitters fire off stress hormones when threatened by a disturbance. Being biological creatures, this will inevitably affect our biochemistry and cause disorder in the neural corridors of cognitive thinking. We all react differently to our environment depending on our diverse background experiences, most especially those retained from when we were young, as this is when we are most vulnerable and dependent on others.

There are certain parts of the nervous system that are likely to influence bipolar disorder. These are:

- The medulla oblongata: This region of the brain contains many important centres of the autonomic nervous system, in particular reflex activities like blood pressure, breathing etc.

- The thalamus: This lies in the middle of the brain and forms an important relay centre, connecting other regions of the brain and assisting in the integration of sensory information. Much of the sensory input received by the brain must be compared to previously stored information before it can be made sense of. The thalamus conveys information received to the appropriate areas of the cerebrum. Pain and pleasure appear to be perceived by the thalamus.

- The hypothalamus: This is the main controlling region for the autonomic nervous system. It comprises two centres, one for the sympathetic nervous system and the other for the parasympathetic nervous system. At the same time, it controls complex patterns of behaviour such as feeding, sleeping and aggression. It also monitors the composition of blood, in particular the plasma solute concentration, giving it a rich supply of blood vessels.

The cerebrum: This performs the functions of receiving sensory information, interpreting it according to information stored from previous experiences and transmitting impulses along motor neurons to allow appropriate responses. It coordinates the body's voluntary responses as well as its involuntary ones. The association areas of the cerebral cortex help an individual to interpret the information received in the light of previous experience.

In psychologist and behavioural geneticist Robert Plomin's book *Blueprint*, on the subject of DNA, he maintains that environmental bumps in our early years affect us but do not last, as we 'bounce back to our genetic trajectory'. Moreover, he believes that we will choose our environments according to our genetic propensities.

Plomin is the youngest president of the international Behaviour Genetics Association and he maintains that whatever we inherit from our parents will become the lifetime source of our personalities – in other words the blueprint of our personalities making us who we are.

Despite what he writes, I still find it hard to entirely banish the notion that upbringing has an effect, at least to some degree, in shaping us to become who we are. But Plomin insists that our parents' rearing influence has little effect on us and goes on to maintain that the genetic inconsistencies we inherit from our parents kick in usually when we reach our late twenties.

Is bipolar disorder linked to intelligence?

I was particularly aware of Leon and Nicky's intelligence at an early age. Leon started to investigate the moon and stars when he was three. A journalist for *The Sunday Times* asked to take him to the Science Museum and subsequently wrote an article about him for *The Sunday Times Magazine* because of his preternaturally high IQ, which was tested at the age of eight. Nicky's nursery school were astonished when he started drawing perfect circles when he was two and his school reports were always phenomenal. I wrote and illustrated a story book when I was around seven, as well as drawing profiles of faces and figures in all the margins of my exercise books. So is bipolar disorder linked to intelligence?

If you pose this question online, you will come across an article entitled 'Genetic overlap between bipolar disorder and intelligence' by postdoctoral fellow Olav B. Smeland and colleagues. Importantly that of the 12 risk genes for bipolar disorder, 75% were also linked to higher intelligence.

This recent study was carried out by NORMENT (Norwegian Centre for Mental Disorders Research) which investigated DNA from more than 400,000 people including 20,000 patients with bipolar disorder and 35,000 patients with schizophrenia.

Another study by Catharine R Gale PhD, G David Batty PhD and Finn Rasmussen PhD found bipolar disorder to be more common in people with exceptionally high intelligence and creativity. Another study suggested that a high IQ in childhood, often resulted in mania in adulthood, although the evidence so far was sparse and there was not as yet enough evidence for either of these assertions to be incontrovertible.

Another indication that exceptionally bright people may be at risk of bipolar disorder comes from findings that boys with very high or very low school grades were both more likely than those with average performance to be hospitalised with bipolar disorder as adults. Whether these associations are driven primarily by intelligence or by other factors that influence educational attainment is unclear.

While the article makes it clear that it is difficult to assess these findings, as high intelligence and bipolar disorder are rare in the community, it maintains that anyone with a high intelligence has an increased risk of bipolar disorder, in it's pure form without any other mental health obstacles.

It would seem natural to assume that anyone with a higher-than-average intelligence quotient is more likely to be overly sensitive and aware and, therefore, be more prepositioned to what are termed as mental problems.

In a more recent study published in the *British Journal of Psychiatry*, a high childhood IQ is linked to an increased risk of bipolar disorder in adulthood. This assertion is made with reference to a number of lead scientists' studies of a large birth cohort – the 'Avon Longitudinal Study of Parents and Children' by the University of Bristol. Researchers tested the IQ of children at the age of eight and then later the same individuals were tested again for manic traits at the age of twenty-two or twenty-three.

The lead author of the study, Professor Daniel Smith from the University of Glasgow, stated that findings from the study had 'implications for understanding how liability to bipolar disorder may have been selected through generations'. He maintains that serious mood problems like bipolar disorder are perhaps the price humankind has to pay for our increased intelligence, our creativity as well as our verbal dexterity.

Smith emphasises that having a high IQ is not a clear-cut factor for bipolar, although it might be an advantage, but perhaps the genes that confer intelligence can get expressed as illness in the context of other risk factors, such as 'exposure to maternal influenza in the womb or childhood sexual abuse'. According to this finding, it seems there are certainly other ways to be imbued with the disorder than simply having it bequeathed to you by your forefathers.

The results are consistent with previous research that suggests individuals with an increased genetic propensity to bipolar disorder were more likely to show a range of creative abilities, especially in areas where verbal proficiency may prove advantageous, such as in literature or leadership roles.

Smith stresses that he hopes the results of research linking high childhood IQ to an increased risk of experiencing manic bipolar traits in later life will lead to more help and improve approaches for the earlier detection of the disorder. Previous studies, it seems, have also found a link between 'creativity' and the risk of schizophrenia and bipolar disorder, as well as a possible association between autism-related genes and higher intelligence.

The eminent German clinical psychiatrist and scholar Emil Kraeplin who was an icon of postpsychonanalytic study believed that increased artistic productivity was more specifically related to manic depression:

The volitional excitement which accompanies the disease may under certain circumstances set free powers which otherwise are constrained by all kinds of inhibition. Artistic activity, namely, may, by the untroubled surrender to momentary fancies or moods, and especially poetical activity by the facilitation of linguistic expression experience a certain furtherance.

An article in *The Guardian* in 2015 reporting on the previously mentioned research by Professor Smith reiterates the idea that the prevalence of conditions like bipolar may be the price we have to pay for our intelligence and creativity. It says:

Individuals who scored in the top 10% of manic features had a childhood IQ almost 10 points higher than those who scored in the lowest 10%. This correlation appeared strongest for those with high verbal IQ.

The results of one recent study suggested that men with high intelligence may indeed be at risk for bipolar disorder in its pure form (without co-morbidity). The association with high intellect might also help to explain why this seriously debilitating condition has been maintained across populations and human history. Another bipolar writer who had researched the topic for 20 years noted that bipolar is attached to a certain type of intelligence, one that is more creative when in a manic state. Otherwise, it appears to present in people who have a higher work ethic, one that is more likely to be intellectual, and pursue a certain professional style of life. If high intelligence and sensitivity go together, couldn't this be likely to spill out into a form of bipolar?

Chapter 3

WHAT DOES BIPOLAR FEEL LIKE?

My first brush with bipolar symptoms came when I was around nine, when I had my first experience of what was thought to be a *petit mal* attack, something my godmother, my Aunt Marion, apparently suffered from. I'd suddenly have the strange feeling that I was walking through a dark and dystopian nightmare. Try as I would, I was unable to recall anything about the enigmatic dream in detail, but it certainly left behind a disturbing feeling of malevolence. Although I remained fully conscious throughout the experience, I was told that the colour drained from my face. These attacks would come and go until my mid-thirties and sometimes last for several days, generally occurring at times of stress or inner conflict. Although I was to have an EEG (electroencephalogram) test, I was informed it was something that was non-organic.

In hindsight I can only imagine it was a part of being bipolar. In time, bipolar would present itself to me as a cyclical state. I would find myself prone to the dismal depressive phase during winter days and only find a release when soaring back into the manic stage when the warmth of the sun once again started to penetrate the dark corners of my mind and my shrammed bones and chilblain-ridden toes. Within a twenty-four-hour period I could switch from my regular winter hibernations to find it impossible to stay asleep in bed for any longer than a four-hour stretch. As the summer temperature rose, I would wake from my slumbers as soon as the morning beams of sunlight fell across my bed, impelled to rise and get on with the joy of living, unwilling to waste a single second more of my valuable time in bed.

Initially the sudden change in my sleep pattern would make me feel nauseous and light-headed, until I became used to it again. Over the following months, I subsequently found I could fall asleep for a brief refreshing nap at any time of the day, sometimes even when sitting up straight on a bench in a gallery where I'd gone to see the paintings. When the seasons changed and the winter decline set in again, I would find myself so exhausted with the long whirlwind of the summer, as well as the overall loss of sleep, that the cycle then set itself in motion once again.

What was going on in my brain to cause such mental volatility wasn't, and isn't, clear. Indeed, there is no computer that can come even close to the complexity of the brain, which weighs a mere three pounds. Hippocrates wrote:

And men ought to know that from nothing else but (from the brain) come joys, delights, laughter and sports, and sorrows, griefs, despondency, and lamentations. And by this, in an especial manner, we acquire wisdom and knowledge, and see and hear, and know what are foul and what are fair, what are bad and what are good, what are sweet and what unsavoury…and by the same organ we become mad and delirious, and fears and terrors assail us. All these things we endure from the brain, when it is not healthy… In these ways I am of the opinion that the brain exercises the greatest power in the man.

The brain, therefore, is without question our most vital organ – and one that is highly vulnerable. It controls all functions of the body and is hidden within a thin skull and composed of the cerebrum, cerebellum and brainstem. Among many other things, it controls our thoughts, memory and speech, movement of the arms and legs, and the function of many organs within our body. I believe our bodies have been largely designed to carry it around. When something is wrong inside the brain, it affects everything.

Bipolar is thought to affect one in 100 people in the UK and is characterised by periods of depression followed by episodes of mania, during which people can feel extraordinarily happy, ambitious and creative. It can also include periods of psychosis. Kay Redfield Jamieson, a foremost authority on bipolar disorder and a professor of psychiatry at the Johns Hopkins University School of Medicine, tells us in her book *An Unquiet Mind* that she is someone who requires regular doses of lithium carbonate to help her survive the more excessive ravages of manic depression. She admits that at times she found her bipolar seductively produced something that was not only the best in our natures but also what is the most dangerous. She also describes it as being intoxicating, pleasurable and allowed a perpetual flow of ideas, and sustained energy.

Bipolar disorder is not a single disorder, but a category of mood disorders defined by the presence of one or more episodes of abnormally elevated mood swings, clinically referred to as mania. Individuals who experience manic episodes also commonly experience depressive episodes or symptoms, or mixed episodes, which present with features of both mania and depression. These episodes are normally separated by periods of normal moods, but in some patients depression and mania may rapidly alternate, known as rapid cycling.

The disorder has been subdivided into bipolar I, bipolar II and cyclothymia, based on the type and severity of the mood episodes experienced.

- Those with type I experience periods of manic highs and depressive lows.

- Those with type II experience severe depression and mild manic episodes – known as hypomania – that last for a shorter period of time.

- Those with cyclothymia experience less severe mood swings, but they can last longer.

- During a manic episode, those with bipolar disorder I, can feel euphoric and have lots of energy, ambitious plans and ideas. But they can become aggressive and experience symptoms of psychosis.

- One in every 100 UK adults will be diagnosed with the condition at some time in their life. Everyone suffers from some form of mood swings, but it is only when it becomes incapacitating that it becomes clinical.

(This information is taken from NHS Royal College of Psychiatrists and Mind.)

To summarise it clinically, bipolar disorder is often a cyclic illness where people periodically exhibit elevated and depressive episodes. According to an online report in 2008:

Most people will experience a number of episodes, averaging 0.4 to 0.7 a year with each lasting three to six months, although some will experience only a single mood episode.

Late adolescence and early adulthood are peak years for the onset of the illness and, as these are critical periods in a young adult's social and vocational development, they can be severely disrupted by its onset.

Symptoms of bipolar psychosis may include the following:

- Disrupted, disorganised or hard to understand speech or thought patterns

- Hallucinations

- Unrealistic beliefs

- Difficulty managing daily activities

- Difficulty knowing what is real and what is not

- Interrupted sleep – especially insomnia or prolonged periods of shorter sleep periods than usual – which can trigger paranoia, particularly during the manic phase when sleep is less than normal or abandoned altogether.

The Royal College of Psychiatrists has recently issued a warning that the Covid pandemic of 2020–21 will result in higher levels of mental illness, which most strongly applies to children. Adrian James, president of the college, describes the situation as 'terrifying. The fact that large numbers of frontline NHS workers are also experiencing anxiety and depression only adds to the severity of the crisis. I imagine many of those isolating for over a year in their homes will also have had the opportunity to appreciate that they have problems with mental disorders they had not had the necessary time to contemplate before.'

It was also reported that many patients during the pandemic experienced 'a lower quality of care' as they were unable to access medication, having appointments cancelled and losing their usual face-to-face help.

But what is it like to suffer from bipolar, or live with someone who does?

Bipolar disorder is one of the most challenging psychiatric disorders to deal with and even, indeed, to explain, being of such a complex nature. As someone who lives with this disorder, the only way I can begin to describe it is that one minute you are sunk in the bleakest depths and the next you are in a manic merry-go-round phase and your brain is cascading with ideas until it spins out of control. These shifts are referred to as 'mood episodes' and there are two main types: manic and depressive episodes – hence the old name manic depression. Each extremity (or polarity) is of equal breadth from the balancing middle norm and it's not unusual for someone to experience the extent of this disorder within the space of any twenty-four-hour period.

During the manic phase, you are too excited to sleep and recharge your batteries, as your mind swirls with a torrent of ideas and plans and your life becomes an endless round of energetic and over-charged activity. You become restless and impatient with other people who you feel are failing to keep up with the speed with which your brain is making connections during your exaggerated mood swing.

Of course, there are various stages of bipolar depending on where you are on the scale. Bipolar I consists of manic episodes lasting seven days or more, which can be severe enough to result in hospitalisation. This stage can also produce dangerous episodes of psychosis. Bipolar II is what is known as hypomania – meaning a less severe episode of the mania and fewer depressive episodes. This appears to be closest to the type of bipolar I believe I suffer from.

There is also the stage of cyclothymia, which again is a less exaggerated series of mood swings. This version of the disorder means you are a little higher or at other times a little lower, rather than the manic-depressive stages of bipolar I or II, but you don't necessarily appear to others to be in a dysfunctional state.

In the manic-depressive swing, the person is either depressed because of a controlling inner tension or else is manic because of being possessed and activated by some aspect of the tense inner situation. During either swing, the person is completely out of touch with the opposite swing of the condition.

Depression is the flip side of bipolar and will not only be equal in its counterbalance to the manic, but prove equally as devastating. As far as the normal is concerned, depression is universal and perfectly common – it is not life threatening in relatively normal adults. But in some, depression can be severe and crippling and can last a lifetime. For a person with bipolar, after a manic phase of being constantly on the go with little relief, your brain runs down like a battery and eventually hits a rock. You feel a sense of dread, and feelings of fear and paranoia overwhelm you. Your confidence fails and feelings of guilt and self-loathing take over until you come to a standstill and life no longer seems worth living. You are looking into the abyss and at such a stage you are liable to contemplate suicide. Indeed, many end up feeling this is the only option.

Others turn to alcohol or drugs to ease the pain, but for me that simply adds another toxic level and one likely to become just another destabilising problem that has to be overcome. There is a total feeling of self-deprecation at its lowest and most egregious vertical descent.

In these periods I would take to blaming myself for the mess I felt I had made of my life, with no understanding of how I was going to get myself back on track again. At such times, my mother's voice rang in my head, reminding me how well I was fulfilling her predictions of my existential inadequacy.

But is bipolar all bad? While I am fully aware of the pain of the depressive state, and the fact that this can prove to be not only episodic but often a serious and considerable disruption to your life, I believe the upside of this disorder has motivated me to do much more with my life, providing as it does a prolonged and vividly heightened awareness without the aid of drugs or a synthetic chemical stimulant. You are full to the brim with youthful vigour, your creative juices are raging and you feel you are reaching into parts of your brain, with all their power of ingenuity, that have hitherto been inaccessible.

It's true I am possibly one of the luckier ones, as my mood swings are less extreme than others, my diagnosis probably being hypomania or cyclothymia, towards the mid-range of the spectrum. I'm aware that such heightened elation has its price, but I've heard of few people experiencing these euphoric 'highs' who would be willing to change their disorder, despite the pain of the inevitable depressions. We may for a time have the chance to experience a multi-coloured world, but we see that as preferable to a monochrome existence – and many of us are willing to pay the price.

The exception to this may be the unfortunate few who suffer the more troubling extremities of this disorder and are prey to the dangerous psychosis that is a symptom of bipolar and requires the use of regular medication. Manic depression illness is closely linked to major depressive or unipolar illness and these depressive symptoms include apathy, lethargy, hopelessness, sleep disturbance (too much or too little sleep), slowed down physical movement and thinking, impaired memory and lack of concentration. It is also capable of dulling all the normal pleasures of life. Suicidal thoughts become the norm and self-blame, inappropriate guilt and recurring morbid thoughts can take over, creating significant interferences to the normal functions of life.

There are many celebrity personalities these days who claim to suffer from bipolar, which for some might appear to add a certain exciting frisson to their star quality due to its possible link to creativity and the disregard for the usual rules of bourgeois conventionality. But if they were to experience the more extreme effects of this disorder, they might think rather differently.

Professor Jamieson, head of psychiatry at the Johns Hopkins, University of Medicine, describes how her own life has been heightened by the disorder and explains how she has lived and loved at a faster pace due to its effects, while the intensity of it has given her a different perspective on life and tested the limits of her mind and background. The fact that she has experienced a different level of sensuality, thinking and feeling she feels she owes to her bipolar disorder.

But she also describes her heartbreak when her doctor advised her not to become pregnant because her illness was so severe that she couldn't afford to come off her medications for any length of time in order to prevent harm to her baby.

Her book *Touched with Fire* is also a memoir to many of her patients and examines manic depression from the dual perspectives of the healer and the healed, revealing both its terrors and its cruel allure. One particular patient refused to take the lithium drug prescribed to him and the disorder eventually cost him his life. She writes about the dreadful effect it had on her although admitting that there are limits to what anyone can do.

She also describes how the disease nearly killed her as it kills thousands of others every year and most of those people are young and among the most creative and gifted in society. Their deaths she feels, are entirely unnecessary.

It's true that many creative geniuses, actors, writers and artists will encounter this phenomenon, since their tendency to have a wider breadth of perception and sensitivity gives them the benefit of a deeper intuitive experience of life. However, it can be a distinctly lonely existence because others cannot accompany them on their lofty flights or their conversely devastating dives. One study seems to indicate some bipolar personalities display an increased striving for attainment of goals and achievements, maybe due to the fact that people with this condition find that being creative is the only way they can communicate to others the intensity of their emotions.

A person with the disorder is generally typified as having a fiery temper and bouts of volatile irritation, dark moods and glimpses of mercurial and irrational behaviour – this being the common view of the artistic temperament. But this view of bipolar is not necessarily a true one. Not everyone with bipolar feels the need to lash out at other people. Having a low boredom threshold myself, once I've reached my goal and proved something to myself, I usually need to move on. Trying to accomplish that perfect work of art, with the inability to ever be truly satisfied for long with your creation, makes for the perfect challenge, one that retains my interest and motivates me further.

Anthony Storr, in the introduction to *Images of Destruction,* further describes the thirteen-year-old Wigoder's experience of the illness as being exhuberant and confident which enabled him to work long and hard during his high periods, resulting in his firm allowing him to lead them into adventurous ventures. But during his low moods he felt emotionally handcuffed. This resulted in his embezzlement of client's fees, a crime he intended to confess to, but instead he attempted suicide. He further attacked his wife with a garden tool, when asleep and ended up being imprisoned, although his wife survived. When he was released, he attempted suicide again. He eventually joined a therapy group where he was able to come to terms with his disfunctional past family life and where he was to meet his next wife,

Suicide attempts are, unfortunately, all too common amongst bipolar sufferers, including myself. While I obviously wasn't 'of sound mind' at the time of my attempts, I was in a pretty wretched state. I don't believe I wanted to die; I only had a need to stop the mental anguish in my head, which made me feel I was losing my mind.

However, people with bipolar disorder who might be experiencing a particular agitated inner state in all likelihood appear completely normal to other people. It takes time to learn how to hide what you might be going through from others, but you soon realise that not many people can help with your problems and being miserable around them only adds to your despair. I became particularly frustrated with being told, 'Cheer up, it may never happen' – as if it already hadn't! Also, being bipolar doesn't mean you appear to be 'crazy' in your manic phase, nor overly depressive all of the time, as there can be sufficiently long periods of total normality and happy productivity in between. But a stressful event can certainly trigger the symptoms.

Indeed, those with the disorder are as sane and balanced as anyone else for most of the time. It is only when some underlying scar or trauma is triggered that symptoms can come to the fore, causing loss of sleep and the mind to become confused and lost, frequently leading to a depression or a manic phase. With bipolar disorder your emotions are always close to the surface and can be easily and disastrously aroused. Once aroused and brought to the surface, they are hard to damp down again.

Sylvia Plath, a well-known sufferer from the condition who took her own life at the age of thirty, characterised her psyche as being 'run by two difference electric currents, one positive and joyful and the other negative and despairing. The one that is running at the time is the one that becomes the dominant force of her life.'

This short passage appears to me to be an eloquent description of bipolar disorder and one I feel that perfectly describes the double life that a person with the disorder finds themselves, at times, forced to live. At one time, I discovered I had two distinct wardrobes: bright colours for the summer days when I was high and dark clothes for winter when I was usually depressed.

Indeed, as an adult, for many years I still particularly dreaded the long dark, winter months and the worsening of the weather, when I would again be drawn down into a depression, only able to issue monosyllabic utterances to anyone who tried to communicate with me. Then when summer came around again my mood could change, sometimes quite dramatically overnight, making me feel for a time nauseous with the lack of sleep, until I was able to hit my stride and get used to it all over again. Not only would the metamorphosis reignite my creativity, but it would allow me to feel socially responsive once more.

My mother, who seemed to find me so difficult, would one minute be telling me, 'For goodness sake, Judy, cheer up. You're making everyone miserable,' and the next calling me 'All of a sudden Judy!' when I'd suddenly be off and out, with my energy brimming over and feeling like I had rapidly stepped over onto a parallel universe that caused me to cast caution to the winds.

By the age of fifteen, I had attended six different educational institutions, none of which appeared overly impressed by my scholastic efforts. One was a convent, which at the time of expelling me told my parents that I was 'a bad influence' and another was a school where a rebellious group had apparently been called by the staff 'the Judy Channell gang', ignominiously naming it after me. It was hardly surprising then that my parents had given up any ambitions for me to become academic and had eventually and grudgingly agreed for me to have an interview at Richmond School of Art. This was the only subject I really enjoyed, and I regularly filled the margins of my exercise books with sketches rather than paying attention to lessons.

All I ever wanted to do was escape the tedium of boring lessons and get out into the open air –especially during the summer weather when I felt particularly stifled and claustrophobic being shut in a dark and dreary classroom indoors. At this stage, I was probably already showing signs of the restlessness that is a familiar symptom of bipolar disorder, also no doubt finding it difficult to concentrate during intermittent bipolar mood swings.

From the folio of sketches I produced at my interview at Richmond School of Art when I was fifteen, I was accepted immediately as a student, and they told me they felt I had a talent best suited to an illustration course. I was, of course, more than overjoyed, but my parents, it seemed, were otherwise. 'You're too young. You haven't finished your formal education yet, and you obviously don't have the confidence to be suitably assertive enough to ever make a living out of art,' I was witheringly informed by my mother. She added, 'You'll just end up poor and painting in an attic. Anyway you need to work for your exams first,' as though I was likely to have much success with them.

Presumably, it didn't occur to my parents at the time that I wouldn't be accepted on an art course until I was some years older and had finished my formal education. But feeling sufficiently denigrated by their lack of encouragement I resigned myself to a humdrum two-year secretarial course at a local polytechnic college. My mother told me, 'Of course, if you still want to do an art course when you have some qualifications under your belt, you can always do that afterwards.' But by then my confidence had been somewhat quashed.

However, my mother had other ideas and now had ambitions for me to compete with my cousin Pamela who had just completed a secretarial bi-lingual French/English course. She was always in competition with her sister-in-law, my godmother, Marion – even going so far as to include the previous year's Christmas cards just to prove she was the one who had the most friends. Thus she then got the idea that when I reached seventeen, I should do an exchange with a French family in Brittany whose son was my age so that I could learn the language.

Plans were made and in due course a photo of him was received in the post looking every inch the young demure schoolboy. This was to be my first solo trip abroad and, after a night spent in my cabin, the ferry gently glided into the ancient harbour of St Malo at dawn the next day. I was enchanted with my first view of a foreign land: a bright scene of scattered outlying rocks dotted around the area of the bay, glimpsed through the suffused glow of swirling mist and the growing soft radiance of the encroaching sunrise.

Even more exciting was the young man who greeted me when I alighted from the train at St Nazaire station later that morning. This was not the serious little schoolboy I'd seen in his school photo – Jean-Pierre was one very attractive and confident young man. Of course I found him appealing – I was seventeen, I was free for the first time in my life and I was in a very foreign land – and he, naturally, was full of Gallic charm.

The family ran a yogurt dairy, something I didn't care to try as I have never liked the smell of sour milk. Every evening after dinner the rest of the family, being early risers, would disappear to bed and Jean-Pierre and I would be left to our own devices. Eventually came the day when we were entirely alone in the flat and he caught me in a bedroom and as good as raped me.

Jean-Pierre then visited me in England, where our 'relationship' continued. But despite Jean-Pierre promising my parents before he left, 'I will come back, and marry wiz her,' I never really believed I'd see him again, or even had any particular desire to.

But this was to be my first experience of being stirred up emotionally, and it made me realise how being in love can have the immediate effect of lifting you from your usual feelings of low life expectations, at least for a time. It's why we all love being in love, a transitory experience at best, but one that temporarily lifts us out of ourselves and our routine default dispositions, which is something I believe all humanity has a tendency to suffer from.

By the age of eighteen, my parents started loosening some of the bonds that bound me and granted me some freedom. By then I had a job in London, which was where I met Mike at the Whisky A Gogo club in Wardour Street. He was to play a serious part in my life. When I introduced my good-looking, 6'3'' boyfriend to my parents one weekend, my mother remarked, 'What a smasher.' She wasn't usually known for her prescience.

My father, having at last woken up to my existence, at least appeared to approve of Mike, after he had found little to praise about my previous boyfriend. Apparently he became upset when I began arriving home late after partying with Mike, but this was something he never approached me about, preferring, it seems, to take it out on my mother.

When I first met him, Mike was deeply unhappy, not only with his life but with his work situation. Being creative and highly intelligent, he obviously needed something more satisfying and fulfilling. Although I became somewhat obsessed with him in the early days, it was often difficult to keep the relationship on an even keel and after a few years I decided to put some space between us and spend some time working abroad. I chose an au pair position in Tripoli in Libya, prior to the reign of Colonel Gaddafi.

Although it was an incredible and enlightening trip travelling overland to North Africa, through France to Rome and then on to Naples, where I picked up a ticket for a ferry boat via Sicily and Malta, Libya itself proved to be quite a shock to the senses of a nineteen-year-old provincial girl like myself.

While enjoying the sights, sounds and smells of such a different culture, I stuck it out for around six months. I was expected to share a bedroom with a small baby and take on some of the household chores for the young London couple who were my employers. The baby's father was a captain in the Irish Dragoon Guards, which were currently stationed in Tripoli, while the mother presumably preferred to carry on working rather than stay at home with her baby son.

When Mike accused me of being unfaithful to him in Africa, although there had been no talk of our becoming engaged, my mood became particularly low and I began to worry about losing my patience with the small baby that I was now spending twenty-four hours a day caring for.

Apart from that, I certainly enjoyed being taken out on my days off by various men friends I had met from the regiment. They would take me to explore the extraordinary sights of Libya, such as the awesome ruins that had been left by the Roman occupation at Sabratha or on trips inland to experience the breath-taking views of endless miles of barren desert stretching beyond the historic and dusty sand-blown city of Tripoli. On one occasion I went for a thrilling horse ride at sunset.

When I returned to the UK, I found it hard to acclimatise to the dark dreary month of November after the brilliant skies of Africa. Mike and I finally became engaged, although he had clearly shown little trust in me when he accused me of carrying on affairs when I was abroad. It turned out that he had spent a lot of time with my parents while I was away, even going on holiday with them the previous summer. But the stress of searching for a more satisfying career, adding to his paranoia about me while I was away, obviously took a heavy toll on him and became apparent when he began to have panic attacks every time he tried to leave his home.

Mike's doctor eventually suggested a spell at Roffey Park mental hospital in Horsham, where he was treated with a new kind of drug called LSD (lysergic acid diethylamide), which was at the time being tested on the in-patients as if they were lab rats. Its effect on the patients was to give them terrifying and extreme – if not life-changing – experiences, for which they received nothing in the way of therapy to help them process and assimilate their recently unearthed, archaic fears. For Mike, it was to change him from someone who would walk away depressed if something triggered his anxiety, into a volatile man who would suddenly become abusive and strike out physically.

While his former behaviour of bottling up his emotions and walking away might have proved less of a release for him, his new behaviour of violent, displaced anger was to prove disastrous for his relationships, including ours. When I talked to his doctor before he left the hospital, he also warned me that Mike had a devious personality.

For me, it wasn't until we were married that I began to experience the more violent side of the charming, witty and attractive man I thought I'd been lucky enough to marry. Although Mike had by now found his vocation as an industrial designer, it's fair to say there were many stresses about to be heaped on his shoulders. It was a boost to his confidence when, as a student, he was invited to start up a business with his former tutor at the college. He then won a bursary on the course, which also helped to get him on his feet again.

When his original partner left to go abroad, Mike's brother, who had followed him onto the same design course, joined forces with him as a partner in the business, and their hard work set them up in a successful design partnership, with Mike as the front man. He and I were by then renting the top floor of an old cottage near the centre of town on a sought-after site on Haven Green in Ealing.

In the meantime, I had an interesting job in Berkeley Square in the heart of the West End of London working for a prestigious advertising agency, J. Walter Thompson. As it was a large company, I was able to work my way steadily through various PR, art and TV departments. Of course, I particularly enjoyed working in the art department but, not having the requisite art degree, I was given the chance to choose to be transferred to the sought-after TV department and eventually became part of the crew of a number of different location films advertising various products, with film stars including Raquel Welch, Britt Ekland, Elke Sommer and Diana Rigg. The various TV producers I worked with were to set up the different location shoots carried out in Europe, from Sweden to Rome. The last production I worked on was filmed at one of the Orsini castles outside Rome with Ken Russell as director, and ended up being finished at the famous Cinecittà studios in Rome. The ads at that time were still being shot on film as it was just before the age of video.

The company that owned the cottage we lived in had by then gone into liquidation after it was found the land could not be used for property speculation as planned, and the company owner disastrously took his own life after his various businesses failed. When I became pregnant, five years into my turbulent marriage, I was able to pay the down-payment on it with my work pension.

However, the building was in need of much constructional renovation to make it viable as a home. Due to the lack of funds, this was something Mike and I would have to take on ourselves, with the bulk of it being done by Mike.

But Mike was becoming increasingly volatile. Before I realised I was pregnant, I had prepared a dinner for friends for which Mike hadn't bothered to turn up. When he finally showed up and I complained about his manners, he lost his temper, throwing furniture around and pushing me down the stairs. I had no choice but to seek a bed for the night with friends nearby and later discovered I was pregnant at the time. I was lucky I hadn't lost the baby – my first son. Mike offered no apology when I returned and he behaved as though nothing had happened, which was to become his usual pattern of behaviour for the future.

Although the birth of our son was a momentous time for both of us, with Mike excitedly staying with me during the birth, after a few more years of his erratic and tempestuous behaviour I fled with my two-year-old son to live with my parents for six months. While I was away, Mike became more financially successful and, thinking it might have changed him, I eventually returned, but only to more of the same irrational behaviour. This worsened when larger structural restoration work started on the house and he discovered I'd had an affair with someone I'd met while on a short break with my son and my sister in Majorca.

Lance, with whom I'd enjoyed a short relationship, was from Johannesburg in South Africa, and by the time I returned to Mike he was on the west coast of America, having continued on his adventurous journey after going through a divorce. He was to return two years later on a business trip to try to persuade me to go and live with him in South Africa, when I was once again seeking a second divorce from Mike. As before, I was not looking for another long-term relationship and by then had decided I had no wish to ever marry again.

It seems fair to say my husband was suffering from some kind of mental disorder, possibly bipolar or BPD (borderline personality disorder – another variant of the disorder), or maybe even both. It's hard to see where one starts and the other ends. He steadfastly refused to accept any aberration in his behaviour or seek treatment, but he obviously experienced some kind of psychosis when it came to his abusive and violent behaviour towards me.

The Oxford dictionary of Psychology states that psychosis is 'Any mental disorder characterised by delusions and/or prominent 'hallucinations' with or, in the narrowest definition of the term, without insight into their pathological nature. Broader definitions include mental disorders characterised by other positive symptoms of schizophrenia such as disorganised speech or catatonia. In older psychological and psychiatric literature, mental impairment grossly interfering with the capacity to meet ordinary demands of life, or gross impairment in reality testing. From the Greek *psyche* mind + osis indicating a process or state.'

It also equates bipolar at its worst with schizophrenia, as they can both morph into similar symptoms at different stages.

In his book *The Divided Self,* the psychiatrist R.D. Laing talks about psychosis being a lifting of the lid on the false self which has been attempting to maintain normality, but has failed to be a fair representation of the truth of the inner self.

This could explain what I experienced with Mike's behaviour when, perhaps having made some innocent request, I would without warning find myself facing a huge over-reaction from him. He would shout paranoid remarks in my face, presumably seeing me as someone else in his delusional state. This is sometimes termed as a displaced anger situation. He would become overly aggressive, sometimes raining down blows to my head with his clenched fists while continuing to shout obscene remarks. When an imposingly tall man like Mike loses his temper it's pretty frightening, but I had my own anger issues and wasn't about to be undermined, so I frequently stood my ground, not realising that you cannot argue with someone when they are in the grip of that type of madness.

Laing, when explaining someone in this type of psychotic state, says that it is important to recognise the delusion that the person is under, and not see them as absurd. When a person is in the grip of a psychosis they are likely to sincerely believe that their parents or their partner is trying to kill them, annihilate them or take over their mind and their soul. He later explains, 'a person's fantasy figures might stay the same or become modified and idealised – or even conversely become more persecutory.'

In Mike's case, he would certainly become more persecutory if I'd been away from him for a time. This ranged from his accusing me of being unfaithful when I was an au pair in Africa to times when I was just having a conversation with another man. He obviously had quite serious 'abandonment' issues as well as being aggressively over-possessive.

Mike, like myself, had grown up during the war, although having been born three years before it began, would have been even more aware of it than me. During the war, his father had become ill with spondylosis, a condition that slowly curves the spine and threatens to crush the organs. Mike's mother subsequently become over-reliant on her eldest son for consolation and emotional support. Mike was highly intelligent, over-sensitive and, of course, far too young to shoulder such a heavy burden.

Although Mike would appear to everyone to be a strong and reliable type, always good in a crisis and happy to help his friends, his mental health was fragile and explosive, especially with regard to the needs of his family. After a scene, there would be no acknowledgement that anything amiss had taken place, neither would there ever be an apology for his disturbing and destructive behaviour.

I was to quickly learn that bipolar rage can be intense and highly erratic – anything can trigger it into an impulsive, violent and explosive rage. A simple request can be responded to with irrational and explosive anger. It is lashing out for no logical reason, even on those that you love and who care for you. It requires no rationality to set it off and it cannot be reasoned with when in full flow.

When I left Mike for the second time, having by now given birth to my younger son, Nicky, I had nowhere to go where we were welcome. My parents agreed to take us in, but reluctantly.

They insisted that my sons – their only grandsons – stay in the upstairs bedroom whenever they were in the house.

Once again I would break down with the stress of having no permanent home we could call our own or even any future possibility of such, since Mike insisted on contesting the divorce once more, essentially prolonging it indefinitely.

After finding it impossible to stay any longer with my parents, we moved in as lodgers with a family, which proved equally unstable, and I was eventually informed by my solicitor that I had every right to return to my former home, especially as Mike was on a long motoring holiday with his friend traversing America. When he returned and found out we had been living like nomads, he generously offered to move out so I could have somewhere to live with the boys. This was a promise he never carried out, of course, and probably never intended to, but by then I was too numb and suffering with an exhaustion that made me too weary to care.

Of course, it was easy for me to blame Mike for all my problems, but although I was approaching my forties, in truth I still hadn't faced up to having problems of my own. It was much easier to concentrate on my husband's – a somewhat dubious exchange.

We were informed by his school that my elder son Leon was finding it hard to concentrate and had been referred to the local child guidance clinic. We had by then discovered that our son had a genius-level IQ and had been named as a 'gifted child', so it wasn't due to any lack of brain power – in fact, probably quite the reverse. His lack of concentration was likely to be as much down to boredom, something bright kids are likely to encounter, coupled, no doubt, with the disturbances going on at home. As his parents, we were asked to attend a session with a child guidance counsellor at the local clinic. While I continued to keep my weekly appointments, my husband decided to attend only the first one. After seeing the counsellor for a while, she suggested that my problems went deeper than she could help me with and she gave me a list of professional analysts for me to contact. It was in an attempt to change myself in order to try to salvage my marriage that I contacted Dr Snow.

My efforts to change in order to fit in with my coercive husband were to no avail. When Mike put his hands around my neck during an argument, I realised the danger I was in if I stayed, and I made sure to show my doctor the marks on my neck as proof of his actions. My analyst, Dr Snow, now strongly recommended I once again instigate divorce proceedings, this time for the third and final time. I had already taken Mike to court by this time and been granted a non-molestation order, which meant that since he had now broken each and every stipulation on the order, I was able to threaten him with further court proceedings. He now had little choice but to move out of the house and live elsewhere.

This time the divorce was granted in the high court and I was given custody of my sons, who were now nine and twelve, and money from my share of our former home to find somewhere we could finally live more peacefully. By this time I believe we were all suffering from PTSD (post-traumatic stress disorder), which is an anxiety disorder caused by being assailed with overly stressful, frightening or distressing events.

So, by this stage in my life, I had experienced the symptoms of bipolar both as a sufferer and an observer. I am not sure what poses the greater challenge. I certainly know that whenever I'm on a manic 'high', I can sense that others can become impatient and annoyed with my grandiose ideas and soaring ambitions. Indeed, people in the manic state of bipolar can be highly irritating and exhausting to others, as their energy levels ramp up and appear to take all the air out of the room. For years that realisation would leave me with the lonely feeling that something I'd said wasn't acceptable or that I just didn't fit in – I was, therefore, a misfit and destined to be out in the cold.

The most dangerous aspect of being in denial about bipolar is that you will be neurotically convinced that everyone is conspiring against you. With bipolar, delusions of grandeur are common during episodes of mania. If a person with the disorder is in the grip of a manic episode, they are also likely to experience delusions, believing they are invincible or have special powers or towering talents. Irrational thoughts are often also characteristic of this disorder, causing fast speech and rambling thoughts, which are hard to follow as they move from subject to exuberant subject, often losing track of their train of thought. At the same time, the sufferer may not be aware that their behaviour isn't consistent with what is actually happening. They may not recognise that their hallucinations or delusions aren't real or notice that other people aren't experiencing them and, when they don't get the reaction they expect, they become paranoid and start to believe they are being unfairly undermined.

So, in a depressive episode, people with bipolar may have feelings of guilt or inadequacy, and in a manic situation they may experience delusions of grandeur. I believe, in some ways, that when you feel paranoid you are likely to project your anger onto someone else in order to release the burden on yourself, but in so doing you isolate yourself at a time when you most need support.

But there are positives that come with the condition. The manic stage of bipolar produces an arousing cascade of chemicals that the neurotransmitters need to uptake, such as serotonin, dopamine and noradrenaline, which is a biogenic amine and crucial to the maintenance of alertness, drive and motivation. The neurotransmitters in turn communicate with the nerve impulses across the synapses of the brain, thereby inducing a heady cocktail of chemicals often compared with the intoxicating feeling of being in love.

For a time at least I would feel highly privileged to experience a state that was akin to the feeling a Buddhist might call 'enlightenment'. However, it may not feel like a very secure place when your head is abuzz with ideas careering around chaotically and everything surrounding you irritates you because it isn't keeping up, including not only other people but inanimate objects that annoyingly refuse to move themselves at your speed.

Despite all of this, at times the exhilarating experience feels like you are euphorically walking on air. Who would want to forego such an out-of-this-world, heady feeling, even if the pay-off is usually dire and even dangerous? It's been suggested that we love being in love because the feeling has the ability to lift us from our usual pensive dispositions and then, when we lose that love, we inevitably fall back into our default state of negativity and anxiety. This kind of black and white thinking is what depressed people exhibit because their fearful brain operates on a 'fight or flight' response.

It was also this experience of the intense highs that led me to my most productive periods of creativity. Was creativity a way out of my thoughts and feelings, a necessary expression of my energy and frustration? Or was the creative brain one of the causes of my condition? These questions led me to explore further the connection between creativity and bipolar.

Chapter 4

BIPOLAR AND CREATIVITY

Creativity was always in my DNA. I was born a fiery and impulsive Aries and, as I later discovered, also under the Chinese sign of the Golden Dragon – a sign that apparently imbues one with a volcano of emotions, as if I needed any more. In the *Handbook of Chinese Mythology* by Theodora Lau, the author introduces the Dragon's personality as being one of mighty magnificence, suffused with mythical folklore. The dragon is apparently enchanting and inspiring. Illusionary or not, those born under the sign display some of its magical properties.

It would seem obvious that I'll have my work cut out trying to live up to that!

When I was about nine, my parents became friendly with a couple in our road who had three children, the youngest of whom was Susie, who was my age and became my friend. When they moved to a larger house up on the hill, I would often go and play in their beautiful, extensive home.

One day I wandered up to the top floor and happened to glance into the bedroom of Mary, the eldest of the three children. Across the room, on an easel, I spied a mesmerising and delicately coloured drawing of a ballet dancer. Catching that picture in a shaft of sunlight from the window that day was a moment of epiphany for me, and one that was to be of significant inspiration for my own artistic life to come.

It wasn't until much later that pursuing art and painting became an obsession, and it was this that caused me to seek out time spent in the Maritimes, where I was ultimately to buy two houses. I wonder now whether the energy and focus I found to renovate and winter-proof these houses was probably also a part of my creative drive.

It was my second analyst, Simon, who encouraged me to start painting; not in the watercolours I had found so insipid at school, but in oils – the glorious colours and textures that I was now about to discover. For me, it was a revelation that was to send me on to dizzying 'highs': finding myself once again too excited to sleep for long and getting up immediately a beam of sunlight appeared through my curtains to search for canvas and oil paints. From dawn onwards throughout the summer months I'd work on my latest subject, producing stark pictures of faceless men and slithery serpents as well as burgeoning and eerie-looking flowers and plants. No doubt these were a gift to any psychoanalyst who might have even the slightest grasp of the theories of Sigmund Freud.

When I was teaching art later, people would often say to me, 'I can't even draw a straight line.' Of course, a straight line is something no artist would particularly wish to produce, unless you are an architect or a draftsman, since only man-made edifices are straight. I've always assured people that anyone can draw if they decide to put their mind to it and develop the craft. When we're born, I insist, it's something that comes with the set.

Some studies have suggested a significant correlation between creativity and bipolar, but the relationship between them is still unclear. One study seems to indicate that bipolar promotes an increased striving for the attainment of goals and achievements. Why else would a person expend so much energy in a creatively taxing way to communicate, if not driven to do so?

For me, being on a 'high' would make me feel especially privileged to be in a place where I could encounter that extraordinary state of enlightenment. It may not be a very secure place on that giddy rung of a ladder, as unconsciously you're aware it can't last, but the views are wondrous and it is a place where time and conventional reality are no longer a consideration.

I am always reluctant to call bipolar an illness because I feel that being over-sensitised to so much more has hugely liberated me to do more with my life. I'm certain that it has allowed me to experience an uninhibited and heightened awareness without the aid of hallucinatory drugs or other such substances. Perhaps I am fortunate that my mood swings are less severe than some others who have had the disorder thrust upon them. I'm also well aware that such heightened elation also has its downside, but I've heard of other people who have experienced these states who would also be unwilling to change. People with the disorder may live at times in a colour-saturated world, but even having glimpses of that heightened state is preferable to a bipolar person than their usual humdrum, monochrome existence.

Graham Greene famously wrote; 'Sometimes I wonder how all those who do not write, compose or paint can manage to escape the madness, the melancholia, the panic and fear which is inherent in the human situation.'

All human life has to find its way to obtain the right kind of nourishment from the environment it lives in, to sustain itself and prosper. If these crucially basic needs – like warmth, shelter, food and affection – are not met, she or he can become assailable to mental disorders.

When my sons left home one by one and went their separate ways after eight years of living with me, I found it difficult to cope and became very morose. Eventually, a second suicide attempt found me back in hospital. This time, my ex-husband, Mike, heard about it and stepped up and paid for private treatment, moving me around until my analyst, Simon, finally suggested a beautiful house called Burrswood, which was set in large grounds near Edenbridge in Kent.

I always found that one of the truly overwhelming things about depression is that you are convinced that this is your true default position. You are fully persuaded that there is no way out of it, any other aspirations are null and void, and you firmly believe you are stuck in the dark for evermore.

But when I finally and inevitably emerged again into the sunlight, I picked myself up and found myself an interesting position at Sky TV, which was in the process of getting up and running in a large building. Its new headquarters were about a twenty-minute cycle ride away from me.

I started with great excitement in the graphics department prior to the network going on air. The building was still in construction, with electricians putting the finishing touches to the offices as well as its underfloor wiring systems, which could precariously trip you up at every junction if you didn't watch your step. It would be several months before Rupert Murdoch had Sky up and running, and it haemorrhaged millions every day with nil returns. His total confidence in this scheme was truly amazing. Being also swept up in the whole exhilarating experience and finding the high-flying atmosphere that surrounded me decidedly heady, at someone's suggestion I immediately took it upon myself to start organising a newsletter for the organisation, something I'd written and circulated to TV outlets worldwide while I was at Visnews. I was on such a 'high' that I was not in the least put out when the female manager summoned me to her office and told me she found the whole idea, in her words, 'just bizarre' and promptly cancelled it. Although they offered me a job in another department, I left shortly afterwards, feeling somewhat disillusioned with the whole project.

Several jobs later, when I was finding it increasingly hard to pin down any positions, even temporary ones, a friend suggested I take up an invitation to go and paint on a friend's boat. I had recently got to know Derek, who I met at a party when he was on a visit to the UK and who had moved to Vancouver. It was a good plan, as I had set my heart on returning to Canada one day.

When the time finally came, I decided to travel to Canada via New York, stopping off overnight with the family of a former student there. He had been a bit of a tenant-from-hell of mine for a while, but he had invited me to spend a few nights with his family there so I could spend a day exploring the city before hiring a car and driving up to Boston to catch a coach ride to Canada.

Things, as usual, did not go entirely to plan. I missed my flight from Heathrow to New York and ended up having to be rescued in down-town New York at midnight by my erstwhile young tenant, who was now seemingly on his best and most obliging behaviour. I then drove up to Hartland, Connecticut to view one of my favourite paintings, William Holman Hunt's 'The Lady of Shalott', which had been sold off to America. It was a delight to finally see the painting but I was very disappointed to find this vivid and inspiring painting, which had taken Holman Hunt seventeen years to paint, hanging in a dark space near the back stairs of the Athenaeum art gallery in Hartland, Connecticut.

I then arrived in Boston the next day, only to discover that the coach services to New Brunswick in Canada had recently been discontinued. When I arrived at Boston airport, planning to visit Martin in Fredericton before travelling to Derek in Vancouver, I was informed that I had no credit on my bank card, as I was funding my trip on the rent from my house, which had yet to be rented out to tenants. In the USA, they do not take your credit on your card for granted as they politely do in the UK – they check it cautiously, something I discovered when they refused to accept it for my flight to Nova Scotia.

I made a beseeching call to Martin to beg for a loan for my flight but he initially baulked at the idea, as he told me he was afraid his erstwhile wife, who had recently returned to him, might see it on the bank statements. However, he reluctantly agreed to borrow it and relayed it to me minutes before the last flight left for Yarmouth, Nova Scotia that evening. At the border I then met with an aggressive import officer who held me up so long that I missed my connecting flight and spent the night in Halifax airport, arriving in Fredericton on the morning commuter flight the next day. In the confusion, one of my cases had vanished – for all I know, it may still be circling on a baggage carousel at an airport near you.

But I was on one of my summer 'highs', so all the drama surrounding me on my current peregrination appeared to be par for the course. Even after I had to move motels after being chucked out of the first one with my luggage kept as hostage, I still appeared to find it an interesting experience in the art of survival.

When the police phoned out of the blue to see if I was all right, I thanked them and informed them that my bank manager had kindly visited my savings bank and taken out enough to top up my bank account in London for me. I doubt you would find such a friendly and accommodating bank manager in any bank today. But I think I must have kept my guardian angel on her toes for a bit – something she was going to need to become accustomed to.

While in Canada, I had intended to start doing quick-sketch portraits in the bustling Boyce farmers' market, which sells seasonal produce and crafts. It was the Saturday morning market that I had visited when I'd been staying in Fredericton with Martin two years previously, somewhere we would often visit for their delicious full-on English breakfasts.

On my way into town, when trying to thumb a lift from a passing car, I'd been lucky enough to be picked up by a kind taxi driver called Robert, who drove me into town free of charge and then picked me up at 5am the next morning so I could reserve a suitably prominent place to work in the market doing my sketch portraits. During our conversation driving into town that first afternoon, with me moaning on about the number of married men who deviously play around, he made an astonishing promise: 'I'm going to look after you for the rest of my life.' Although I hardly took him seriously, it turned out he was to keep his promise, although he somehow forgot to tell me that he was also a married man. He later admitted to me that his wife had always warned him: 'Never pick up anyone thumbing a lift.' I was lucky he'd decided to ignore her that day. At the time I dubbed him my 'knight of the road.'

The Boyce Saturday morning market had now grown to more than twice the size. The cafe was now on a large, elevated section of floor overlooking a hall full of indoor stalls selling inviting, locally sourced food produce as well as exquisite craftsmanship work, which now also extended to a large number of stalls surrounding the building outside. The Maritimes is a famous area for gifted artists and craftspeople who take great pride in their work.

In later years, when Robert and I set out our stall, with me doing my quick portraits and him chatting up the queue and then putting the finished picture into one of his ready-made frames, the burger stall next door to us would tell us they substantially increased their sales when we were there. It meant they'd always keep the empty stall waiting for us if we were late of a morning.

After a few weeks, Robert offered to sell me one of his fleet of deluxe taxis and I moved out of town to rent a large and picturesque converted riverside farmhouse with over 100 acres where I planned to paint to my heart's desire. It was slowly dawning on me that my long lost birthright to happiness was alive and well and had been living all the while in Canada.

I felt I had now proved to myself that I could be fully in charge of my own agency and could cope very well with the vicissitudes of life. Not only that, but I was now finding I had certain talents that could sustain me and I wasn't as hopeless as some people in my life had led me to believe. It occurred to me that I could live and I could thrive without the usual dramas that had so far beset and bedevilled my life – something that was an enormously comforting perception. But I still had to deal with an analyst's vexing suggestion that I was self-destructive.

Winter was coming on and it became obvious that it wasn't going to be possible to get my car up the long driveway from my large farmhouse onto the Canadian Highway along the top of the property when it iced up. Not only that but I was running up debts when commissions for portraits dried up. With Robert's help, I hastily moved into an empty house that had been left to him in Newcastle. It was a house he'd helped his father build and where his father had lived until he died the year before.

The house in Newcastle in the north of New Brunswick became a haven for me from debts I had accrued when commissions for portraits had been cancelled after people were advised to tighten their belts financially due to economic problems in Canada. Banks in Canada don't extend credit and will just return cheques if not covered.

By then I had a large dog for company, a handsome and docile retriever/collie that I had discovered at the nearest SPCA. His owner, who had died, had obviously lavished love and patience on him as he was so well behaved. Robert would visit me when he could, in between his visits to his lawyer to sort out his marital finances so he could get a legal separation from his wife. We would enjoy romantic times together when he got the chance to get away and drive the hundred or so miles north to visit me unexpectedly for a few days.

He sold his sky blue Ford Fairlane car that he was so proud of to finance a new boiler for me as he said he didn't want me to freeze in the north if the old one broke down, something I was grateful for as winters in Canada can be breathtakingly cold. Newcastle was the town where Max Aitken, later Lord Beaverbrook, had grown up. It was a small, rather austere town with large grey-stone, Victorian buildings. The Aitken's family were a prominent family in Fredericton, the capital town of New Brunswick, with many important institutions named after them. I was to become involved with one in particular – the Beaverbrook Art Gallery.

After about six months of moving around the Maritimes, it was time for me to return to the UK to see my younger son, Nicky, off on his gap-year journey around Asia. I found work doing market research interviews door to door, which was exhausting but remunerative when I managed to be employed by several companies back to back. Meanwhile, Robert would spend his time commuting month on month thirteen times from Canada to stay with me, until he ran out of the money from the sale of his father's house in Newcastle.

When I returned to Canada again after another eighteen months, Robert and I found our dream log home in a picture-postcard rural setting. The Swiss-style log house needed finishing, as the builders had abandoned it when their building business had gone bust. We immediately set to work on the interior and once again Robert used the sale of his car, a much loved Land Rover, to finance my birthday present: a studio built onto the side of the house, which he employed two builders to erect for me. In the summer we would spend our time attending fairs where I could work doing my sketch portraits while he offered to frame them. We proved to be a good team, and the extra cash went into the restoration of our new home, as well as the yearly commutes back to London to escape the worst of Canada's cold winter months.

Our last Christmas in the UK was when my grandson, Leon's son, was born. Jake was a tiny bundle, as he was born a few weeks early, but I immediately adored him. When I used to go and collect him to take him out for the day he would so remind me of his father, Leon, at the same age that it was as though I was reliving my early days with him, but being so much older and more settled, I seemed able to enjoy them more. It was so hard for me to leave him and return to Canada with Robert that winter, where we hoped to finish our work on the house before enjoying the summer months.

But the idyll was not to last. One cold winter night, a few months later, Robert tragically died of a second heart attack, having already suffered a serious one just before I met him. It immediately plunged me back into another black abyss. I blamed myself for letting him embark on the extensive house renovations when he had a history of angina problems. With a heavy heart, I realised that I couldn't go on living in the former 'dream house' we'd had such plans for and where Robert had died, and I decided I needed to sell up in Canada and return to the UK.

Although a friend came over from London to help me sort everything out and sell up, it was nevertheless hard to get myself going again. After a disturbing experience when I inhaled a strong drug that was offered to me and a doctor had to be summoned to calm me down and stop me jumping off the top balcony, I had to pull myself up from the floor once again and return to the UK.

I had painted Robert's strong features in a portrait a number of times, but one particular painting – a larger-than-life portrait – I had hung on a wall in a bedroom of my house in the UK. One Sunday evening, later that year, I decided to call a friend of his in Canada who, to my surprise, informed me that the last people to buy my log home had sold it because they decided the house was haunted. Feeling completely nonplussed at this unexpected news, I walked upstairs in the gathering gloom to look once again at the painting of Robert I had hung in a bedroom upstairs, and when I turned the light on to look at the portrait, I suddenly felt such a powerful energy coming from it that, in shock, I intuitively stepped backwards in fear and utter surprise.

The next day I obtained the name of a medium from Simon, my analyst, and made an appointment to see her as soon as possible. When I arrived with the painting of Robert, she told me to put it to one side and started telling me, 'He has been trying to get in touch with you for some time to tell you to stop blaming yourself for what happened.' She then continued to describe him in accurate detail. As she spoke, it was hard for me to believe the messages could have been coming from anyone else.

From that moment on, I was on the search for anything that could give me more information about spirituality and metaphysics. When a friend suggested I read Neale Donald's Walsch series of books, *Conversations with God*, at first I was entirely cynical about the idea – God talking to someone? How absurd. But when I saw a pile of the books stacked up in front of me when I next visited Waterstones bookshop in Bath, I decided it could merely be some coincidence or, just maybe, I was supposed to read these books. I decided to put them to the test and bought the first three books. They were to have a huge impact on my thinking. Perhaps I'm gullible, but for me the books were written in such a practical, down-to-earth way that they appeared to validate everything I had ever believed about life and why so much is wrong about the way we think and the way we behave towards each other.

I read and re-read them countless times until they became intuitively entrenched in my philosophy and my way of thinking. In the meantime, I found myself once more employed in London in another uninspiring job, before I decided to let my house again to finance myself on a full-time art course after the one I'd missed out on when I was seventeen. With great excitement and anticipation, I was immediately accepted on an art foundation course at the City of Bath College, free of charge because I was a mature adult. After renting a tiny weaver's cottage for my first year in the West Country, and discovering various friends and cousins living nearby, I decided to sell my London house and found a small, charming cottage perched on a hillside in Bradford-on-Avon, overlooking one of the Wiltshire white horses. I then followed my foundation course by attending an HNC course for a year at the City of Bristol College, before deciding to return to find somewhere to paint again in Canada. This time I was determined to try to depict on canvas what I felt I had learned from the Walsch CWG books.

I was particularly driven to create when emerging from the depths of a depression and later learned that the unconscious holds your imagination and vision. As Theseus heroically emerged from the cave to spread the good news that he'd destroyed the Minotaur, we also want to share with the world what we believe we have discovered in the depths of our minds and portray it in whichever format expresses it best for us. It's possible that bipolar, which by its very nature gives you a far wider breadth of discernment, allows those with the disorder to plumb even deeper into the layers of their unconscious. So the question is: are creativity and bipolar disorder inextricably linked?

The Mad Genius

The Mad Genius is a recurring stereotype of contemporary cultural expression and many famous personalities and creators have suffered from physiological disorders of one kind or another. Creativity and genius may be a sought-after trait; however, it is commonly believed to be associated with mental imbalance. Salvador Dalí said, 'The only difference between me and a madman is that I am not mad.' Whether creativity and madness go together has been questioned since antiquity. Aristotle wrote that the creative act was a natural event and, as such, conformed to natural law. Plato, in contrast, claimed that a poet's inspiration arose during moments of divine madness, but then the Greeks thought that certain mad states were brought on by the gods.

In his book *The Price of Greatness,* Arnold Ludwig, a professor of psychiatry, discusses whether you have to be mad to be creative, stating that those in professions that relate to logic and reason such as architects, journalists and critics are the ones more likely to be less prone to mental imbalances whereas the artists, poets and composers of this world whose work is more inspired by their emotions and vivid imaginations are more likely to be mentally stricken.

He goes on to suggest that people who are unstable cannot fit into normal employment institutions and are more likely to find their way into less organised professions. In other words, there are many who become creative because they are rebels against the system.

Nevertheless, there is a strong compulsion with bipolar people to put in excessive work for any creative project they happen to have taken up, and you might say that that sort of compulsion to work is almost a medical condition of its own. You start to think that if you're not involved in doing this or creating that, you will become incapable of getting out of bed in the morning. Creativity becomes a release for a fevered mind, a divergent activity for whatever chaos is going on internally, because becoming involved in any creative activity immediately takes your mind off anything else.

In the past, schizophrenia and melancholia were among the many forms of mental illness that were seen as the main sources of creativity, while recent research has more emphasised the role of depression and manic mood swings. Research shows that many of those with a disposition for mental problems were suffering with a mental imbalance before their chosen career got them off to a flying start.

For poets, the very act of evoking painful memories from the past – especially ones from the most vulnerable years of childhood – and using them in order to compose something emotive is like playing with fire. It may well be impossible for them afterwards to put the lid back on those strong emotions.

In *Phaedrus and the Seventh and Eighth Letters*, Plato, when discussing artistic 'madness' or possession of the Muses, says:

> If a man comes to the door of poetry untouched
> by the madness of the Muses, believing that
> technique alone will make him a good poet, he
> and his sane compositions never reach perfection,
> but are utterly eclipsed by the performances of
> the inspired madman.

However, when evaluating famous poets who were felt to display forms of mental disorder, be it bipolar disorder or any other mental state, we can obviously only make assumptions from the way they lived their lives as well as their creative output.

Edgar Allen Poe, when writing of poets, held that:

> Aristotle, with singular assurance, has declared
> poetry the most philosophical of all writing –
> but it required a Wordsworth to pronounce it the
> most metaphysical.

He went on to say that:

> Poetry, above all things, is a beautiful painting
> whose tints, to minute inspection, are confusion
> worse confounded, but start boldly out to the
> cursory glance of the connoisseur. We see an
> instance of (Samuel Taylor) Coleridge's liability
> to err by reason of his very profundity and of
> his error to have a natural type in the
> contemplation of a star.

In his long treatise on Poe in his psychopathic study, a certain Dr Robertson suggests that genius (from *genere,* to beget) is inborn. He describes it as an inheritance and the person possessing it being no way responsible for it or it's conclusion, and he felt that it often led to disaster rather than success. He stated. 'All great things are conceived by the man of genius and the cranks turn the world.'

In his book *Art as Therapy*, Alain de Botton says he feels that art can help us go beyond the limits of the capabilities that we've been endowed with, compensating us for some of what we refer to as our psychological frailties.

I believe that many of us paint to remember the things we prize and the people we love, in our effort to try to hold them forever while striving to capture the essence of them. We also paint to help us identify what is central to us but is too hard to articulate in words, language having so many limitations. Some people paint to turn an inspiration into a commodity, since the art scene has now become another branch of the stock exchange. Others paint because they are compelled to communicate in that way, because it's the only way they know how, because they suffer with bipolar disorder or another similar mental health issue.

For me, painting is about communication as well as a way to be in touch with my unconscious, and in the process allow myself to become so wrapped up in it that I forget any of the large or petty problems that might be upsetting me – at least for a space of time. In that way, any creative occupation, be it art or writing, has a therapeutic and healing outcome; it allows us to go within the confines of ourselves and return feeling duly refreshed, with something worthwhile. This seems especially important to anyone who is beset with a mental disorder.

The burning question is, do bipolar disorder and creativity go together? Western cultural ideas of the 'mad genius' and the 'artistic temperament' date back to Aristotle's time when he observed that, 'no great genius has ever existed without a strain of madness.' There has been a wealth of investigations into this area, formal and anecdotal, which have been in support of this view. Overall, these studies suggest a tenfold increase in the rate of bipolar disorder among artists as compared to the general population. The association between creativity and bipolar is well documented in eminently creative individuals, with artists like Vincent Van Gogh and Edvard Munch, authors like F. Scott Fitzgerald and Ernest Hemingway, poets like Walt Whitman and Sylvia Plath and composers like Rachmaninoff and Tchaikovsky to name but a few in some of the most obviously creative categories. All of them reportedly struggled with the illness. Numerous studies have consistently reported an over-representation of affective disorders and psychosis among successful people in creative professions, as well as exceptional creative potential in the relatives of these individuals with bipolar.

However, creativity is not always a bipolar trait, and in a large study of psychiatric patients it was noted that only eight per cent of those with the disorder could be considered to be highly creative. It has since been suggested that the over-representation of bipolar in studies of creativity may only reflect the fact that people suffering with the disorder frequently find it impossible to find permanent jobs or, if they do, find it impossible to hold one down due to their restlessness and fluctuating energy levels. They then have little choice but to lead an unconventional – and quite possibly a chaotic – type of lifestyle.

Some undiagnosed creative temperaments from history

Edgar Allan Poe (1809–1849)

Poe was an American writer, poet and literary critic – hence his comments as previously stated. He is best known for his poetry and short stories, particularly his tales of mystery and the macabre.

Regarded in literary histories and handbooks as the architect of the modern short story, he was also the principal forerunner of the 'art for art's sake' movement in nineteenth-century European literature. In his work he demonstrated a brilliant command of language and technique as well as an inspired and original imagination.

He was only three years old, with an older and younger sibling, when both his parents, who were professional actors, died. His father had already abandoned the family; his mother died of tuberculosis. They had both been members of a repertory company in Boston in America. Poe was then raised in the home of John Allan, a prosperous exporter from Richmond, Virginia, but Allan never legally adopted him. He was educated in the best scholastic establishments, but when admitted to the University of Virginia, he left shortly after because of the lack of funds for his fees from Allan.

It is not entirely clear whether Poe suffered from bipolar disorder, although his writings might indicate a predisposition to the mental disorder when he was described as the 'mad genius' or 'tormented artist'. Many of his bizarre characters would appear to blend with his own personality and the diversity of his interests, be it cryptology or his literary critiques, indicating a restless, yet highly intellectual brain. He is said to have died of a congestion of the brain, although a mystery still surrounds this view. He was only forty years old when he died.

George Gordon, Lord Byron (1788–1824)

Lord Byron was born in London and died in Missolonghi, Greece. Byron was a British Romantic poet and satirist whose poetry and personality captured the imagination of Europe. He was renowned as the 'gloomy egoist' from his autobiographical poem *Childe Harold's Pilgrimage* (1812–18) in the nineteenth century and he is acclaimed for the satiric realism of *Don Juan* as well as his other works. He is regarded as one of the greatest English poets.

George Gordon Byron who was the sixth Baron, was always known simply at Byron. He was the son of Captain (Mad Jack) Byron and his second wife, Catherine Gordon, who was a Scots heiress. After her fortune-hunting and widowed husband, who had a daughter Augusta from his first marriage, had squandered most of her inheritance, she took her infant son to Aberdeen, Scotland, where they lived in lodgings on a paltry income. Captain Byron, having fled to France to escape his creditors, died in France in 1791.

George had been born with a club foot and became extremely sensitive to his lameness from early on. At the age of ten, he unexpectedly inherited the title and estates of his great-uncle William, the fifth Baron, including Newstead Abbey, which had been presented to the family by Henry VIII. Byron subsequently attended school at Harrow public school. In 1803 he fell in love with a distant cousin, Mary Chatsworth, who rejected him since she was already engaged. She was to become, for Byron, the symbol of idealised and unattainable love. When he met Augusta Byron, his half-sister around this time, although she was five years older than him, he is said to have had a close relationship with her. It was suggested it was an incestuous affair

In 1805 Byron entered Trinity College, Cambridge, getting into debt and indulging in the usual vices of undergraduates there. The signs of his bisexual leanings became more pronounced in what he later described as his 'love and passion' for a young chorister, John Edleston. Despite Byron's strong attachment to boys, as in the case of Edleston and his countless affairs with women throughout his life only goes to indicate the strength of his robust heterosexual drive. In 1806 Byron had his early poems privately printed in a column entitled 'Fugitive Pieces' and that same year he formed at Trinity what was to be a close lifetime friendship with John Hobhouse, who stirred his interest in liberal Whiggism.

His first published volume of poetry, *Hours of Idleness*, appeared in 1807. A negative critique of his book in *The Edinburgh Review* initiated his retaliation in 1809 with a couplet satire, *English Bards and Scotch Reviewers* in which he attacked the contemporary literary scene. It was to gain him the first recognition of his formidable talent.

When he came of age in 1809 he took his seat in the House of Lords before he embarked on a tour with his friend, Hobhouse. While in Greece, Byron began *Childe Harold's Pilgrimage*, finishing it when in Athens. Greece made a lasting impression on Byron. While there, he appreciated the Greek's free and open frankness, which for him contrasted strongly with English reserve and it served to broaden his views. He delighted in the sunshine and the lack of hypocrisy and moral tolerance that he was to perceive in the people.

After a series of unconventional relationships, including the one with his half-sister Augusta, which was reflected in a series of gloomy Oriental verse tales he wrote at the time, in 1815 he married Anne Isabella Milbanke, who gave birth to his daughter Augusta Ada. However, the marriage was doomed and their relationship ended, with rumours swirling regarding his bisexuality as well as his womanising. To escape them, Byron fled abroad in 1816, never to return to England.

The statement that Byron was 'mad, bad and dangerous to know' comes from his lover, Lady Caroline Lamb, after their first meeting, when the publication of *Childe Harold* made him the literary and social lion of London at the age of twenty-four. His relationship with her also served to make her a famous historical figure.

He spent time in Geneva near Percy Bysshe Shelley and Mary Goodwin (later Mary Shelley) who is thought to have written the famous story of *Frankenstein* when they all shared a house on the lake. Byron, meanwhile, continued to move around Europe, and was later saved from his profligate lifestyle by a nineteen-year-old countess, winning the friendship of her family, Counts Ruggero and Pietro Gamba, who initiated him into revolutionary plans to free Italy from Austria. He later left his second daughter, Allegra, who was sent to him by her mother Claire Clairmont, in a convent near Ravenna, where she was to die the following April.

In 1823, in his continual search of new adventures, he again became involved in a struggle for independence by the Greeks from Turkish rule. He made efforts to unite the various Greek factions and took personal command of a brigade of soldiers, reputedly the bravest of the Greeks. He was to become a hero to the Greek cause after he helped them become independent from the Ottomans by presenting them with a cheque for £4,000 – roughly £332,000 in today's money. He remains a hero to the Greeks to this day.

But a serious illness in 1824 resulted in him contracting the fever from which he died at Missolonghi in the April of that year. He was still a young man at 36. His body was refused burial in Westminster Abbey, being placed in the family vault near Newstead, although a plaque regarding him was to be placed later in the abbey.

Byron's huge body of writings are thought to be mainly autobiographical and the paradoxical nature of his complex character can be seen throughout them:

> …The mind's canker in its savage mood,
>
> When the impatient thirst of light and air
>
> Parches the heart; and the abhorred grate,
>
> Marring the sunbeams with its hideous shade,
>
> Works through the throbbing eyeball to the brain
>
> With a hot sense of heaviness and pain.

Byron, it appears, was to suffer greatly from his 'predisposition to grief' and often feared that he was going mad – a feeling I can relate to from the worst of my own depressions. He wrote and talked about suicide and, from a medical point of view, lived a lifestyle likely to bring about an early death. His symptoms, family psychiatric history and the course of his illness clearly fit the pattern of manic-depressive illness. His restlessness and sexual promiscuity, proneness to violent mood changes and his need to write creatively, probably saved him from completely losing his mind. While it seems in his case that a disorder of some kind was already well embedded in the family, people with this disorder are often unable to see much beyond their fitful mood swings, and their unabated efforts to control them, which don't usually make them the most considerate or empathetic parents.

Ada, Countess of Lovelace (1815–1852)

Ada, Countess of Lovelace, was the only legitimate offspring of Lord Byron. From her father she inherited a mercurial temperament that swung precipitously from the ecstatic and grandiose to the melancholic. She also acquired the Byron family's disposition for gambling and financial chaos: at one point, after being convinced she had invented an infallible betting system, she was forced to pawn the Lovelace family jewels when her losses on the horses become ruinous. It was in her temperament, however, that she was most particularly her father's daughter. Byron, although living mostly in exile during her childhood, followed his daughter's progress as closely as he could, and noted not long before he died that a description he had received of her character and disposition had prompted him to remark, 'She very nearly follows my own, except that I was more impetuous.' Summing up his view of her, he stated:

> Her temper is said to be extremely violent –
> is it so? – It is not unlikely considering her
> parentage – My temper is what it is – as you
> may perhaps divine – and my Lady's was a
> nice little sullen nucleus of concentrated
> Savageness to mould my daughter upon – to
> say nothing of her two Grandmothers – both
> of whom, to my knowledge were as pretty
> specimens of female spirit – as you might
> wish to see on a Summer's day.

Although she never knew her father personally, she was interested to learn everything she could find about him, although he died in Greece when she was only eight years old.

She was educated privately and was assisted in her advanced studies by prominent mathematicians, a subject she was encouraged to pursue by her mother, who wanted to guide her away from any inclinations towards poetry that she might have inherited from her father.

It was an unusual upbringing for an aristocratic girl at the time, but her mother continually insisted that tutors taught her mathematics and science. This was certainly not on the standard educational curriculum for girls at the time but her mother thought that such rigorous studies would prevent her from developing her father's moody and unpredictable personality and taking up a poetry career. She was also forced to lie still for extended periods of time as her mother believed it would help her develop self-control.

In 1835 she married William King, eighth Baron King, and when he was created an earl three years later she became Countess of Lovelace.

Her grandiose episodes were charged with an energy and power and a hugely confident 'exhilaration of spirit'. She grandiosely even outlined plans for taking on the 'energies of the universe'. So far, so typical, especially of someone experiencing the euphoric stages of the manic side of the bipolar syndrome.

She became interested in Babbage's machines in 1833 when she was introduced to him through her friend, the author Mary Somerville, and in 1843 she came to translate and annotate an article written by the Italian mathematician and engineer Luigi Federico Menabrea. She not only translated the original French text into English, but also added her own thoughts and ideas on the machine. Her notes ended up being three times longer than the original article, being detailed, elaborate and deemed to be excellent. They prompted her to remark, 'The Analytical Engine weaves algebraic patterns just as the Jacquard-loom weaves flowers and leaves.' While Charles Babbage conceived the idea of the Analytical Engine, the forerunner of the digital computer during the mid 1830's Lovelace's contribution, has, of late, finally been recognised. The early programming language 'Ada' was named for her and the second Tuesday in October has become 'Ada Lovelace Day', on which the contributions of women to science, technology, engineering and mathematics are honoured in the USA.

She and her husband had three children and by all accounts her husband encouraged her mathematical aspirations. They socialised with prominent names such as Michael Faraday and Charles Dickens.

After a bout of cholera in 1837 her health suffered, adding to her lingering problems with asthma and her digestion. She was administered painkillers such as laudanum and opium, which brought on a change to her nature. She began experiencing significant mood swings and hallucinations, typical of the mental problem of manic depression.

She had possibly inherited her mercurial temperament from her family, especially from her father, although her mother also appeared mentally unbalanced, certainly in her treatment of her young daughter – her childhood was very different from a normal one. Her moods would swing from ecstatic and grandiose to melancholic in a matter of days or weeks. Bipolar disorder would seem to be the only diagnosis that could be interpreted from such behaviour, especially recalling the Byron family disposition for suicide, melancholy and erratic behaviour. She died aged thirty-six, the same age as her father. Although her contributions to the field of computer science were not discovered and appreciated until the 1950s, she has since received many posthumous honours for her work.

Samuel Taylor Coleridge (1772–1834)

Coleridge was the youngest of fourteen children and his father, who married twice, was a vicar and grammar school master. Coleridge was a student at his father's school and from the start was a keen reader. The Coleridge family was a highly accomplished one, starting with soldiers and scholars and later becoming prestigious judges, bishops and senior academics.

His mother, however, was cold and had little to do with her youngest son, not taking the trouble to visit him even once during his schooling. None of his other family did either. He was left to wander the town alone as he was apparently not even invited to go home during term breaks or school holidays. Perhaps the loneliness he suffered as a child was borne out in his famous poem of the wandering and lonely Ancient Mariner.

When his father died in 1781, Coleridge attended Christ's Hospital School in London where he met Charles Lamb, who was to become a lifelong friend. Another friend, Tom Evans, introduced Coleridge to his family and he fell in love with Tom's sister Mary.

He then began to live a double life at Cambridge, his wild expenditure on books, violin lessons, theatre and whoring (he later described this as the time of his 'unchastities') alternating with fits of suicidal gloom and deep remorse.

By the end of October 1793 his 'embarrassments' regarding his chaotic lifestyle 'buzzed around him like a nest of Hornets' and in November he gave up all attempts to get his affairs under control. Instead he abandoned himself to a whirl of drunken socialising, followed by a downward spiral with grim solitary resolutions to shoot himself as the final solution to his bad debts, unrequited love and academic disgrace. He was never to finish his degree.

Coleridge's father had wanted his son to be a clergyman like himself, so Coleridge made an attempt to please his father by entering Jesus College, Cambridge in 1791, focusing on a future in the Church of England. However, his views changed over the course of the first year and he became a supporter of William Frend, whose Unitarian beliefs made him controversial. While at college, he accumulated large debts, which were to haunt him for the rest of his days.

On meeting Robert Southey, he decided to postpone for several weeks his intentions for a trip to Wales in 1794, to give the two men the opportunity to share their philosophical views. They were to be influenced by Plato's views in *The Republic* and discussed a vision of equal government for all called pantisocracy, which, they decided, involved moving to Pennsylvania in America, to the banks of the Susquehanna River. The plan was to set up a new world there with a great library, philosophical discussions and freedom of religious and political beliefs – but it was another plan that was never to come to fruition.

When Coleridge returned from Wales, he found his friend Southey had become engaged to a certain Edith Fricker and, as communal living was part of their future plans for their perceived new world order, Coleridge decided with Southey's persuasion to marry her sister Sarah. But by then Southey had defected from the pantisocratic scheme, leaving Coleridge married to a woman he didn't really love. Worse, he was still in love with Mary Evans, who was now engaged to another man. His marriage, consequently, was not a happy one and he spent most of the rest of his life separated from his wife. If his work suffered as a result of this, one explanation could be because he now found he had to reconcile his intellectual aspirations with the financial needs of his family, which turned out to be something he consistently failed to do. In 1795 Coleridge met William Wordsworth, who was to have much influence on his writing, which then became more natural in style. Together, the two men entered upon one of the most influential creative periods of English literature. The following year Coleridge used many of his friends in his 'conversation poems', along with his own experiences.

From 1797 to 1798 he lived near William Wordsworth and his sister, Dorothy, in Somerset, where the two men collaborated on *Lyrical Ballads*, a collection considered to be the first great work of the Romantic school of poetry and which also contains *The Rime of the Ancient Mariner*, a depiction of a lonely wanderer on the wild seas of life that is probably his most famous poem. The work they achieved together lifted Wordsworth from a depression he was experiencing at the time due to recent events. He has since been considered to be another sufferer of a certain mental disorder.

In the autumn, the two poets travelled to the Continent together, where Coleridge mastered the German language, which he then began translating. On his return, he settled in Keswick with family and friends and over the next two decades lectured on literature and philosophy. He spent two years on Malta as secretary to the governor to try to ease his addiction to opium, living off financial donations and grants.

Having at one time retired to a lonely farmhouse near Culbone in Somerset, Coleridge composed, under the influence of laudanum, the mysterious poetic fragment known as *Kubla Khan*. The exotic imagery and rhythmic chant of this poem have led many critics to conclude that it should be read as a 'meaningless reverie' and enjoyed merely for its vivid and sensuous qualities. An examination of the poem in the light of Coleridge's psychological and mythological interest, however, suggests that it has a complex structure of meaning and is basically a poem about the nature of human genius. The first two stanzas show the two sides of what Coleridge elsewhere calls, 'commanding genius' and 'its creative aspirations in time of peace'. In the final stanza, the poet writes of a state of 'absolute genius' in which, if inspired by a visionary 'Abyssinian maid', he would become endowed with the creative, divine power of a sun god – an Apollo or Osiris – subduing all around him to harmony by the fascination of his spell. He was to be nicknamed 'the little genius' by later generations for these types of grandiose aspirations.

There followed a falling out with Wordsworth when he fell in love with, and was later rejected by, the sister of the woman Wordsworth was to marry, and this was to become the darkest period of his life. Opium retained its powerful hold on him, but in spite of this he became fashionable in London and delivered a series of lectures, which attracted a large audience. He became interested in William Shakespeare and his play *Osorio* was produced at Drury Lane in 1813.

He had become addicted to opium, and after moving in with James Gillman in 1816, he wrote more of his lyrical poems. But before he died, he became an advocate of Christianity, something he was to find greatly comforting as it seemed to offer him a way of life that he would find supportive. It was to become his official creed, which would help his relationships with orthodox Christians, not only giving him some social standing, but enabling him to pursue his former intellectual explorations in the hope of reaching a Christian synthesis that might help revitalise the

English Church, both intellectually and emotionally. He died in London in 1834.

Although it seems the family suffered from manic depression, perhaps they were not as seriously affected as the Byron dynasty. Nevertheless, Coleridge's grandfather was later described by him as 'half-poet, half-madman' and was to also experience bankruptcy and become a heavy drinker. Coleridge's older brother Francis committed suicide at the age of twenty-two and Hartley, Coleridge's son, also showed signs of manic depression and struggled with alcoholism while still at university, and was as a consequence sent down from Oxford.

Others appeared to be overly attracted to Coleridge, despite his obvious mental disorder and the extremity of his mood swings. Many of his friends appeared happy to help him financially, often taking him in to live in their own houses. Perhaps he had a need to find an alternative family ambience, having been treated so coldly by his own, something I can certainly relate to. But he was never able to settle for long anywhere and his opium addiction no doubt shortened his life.

Having known his present namesake, the current inheritor of the famous name and a direct descendent, I can attest to the fact that the Coleridge charm still survives, as well as the restless spirit.

Sara Coleridge (1802–1852)

The only daughter of Coleridge was also a writer and poet like her father and had published two books by her early twenties. She was close to her father in her work as well as in her personality. In similar fashion, she also suffered from severe depression, recurrent hysteria and nervousness and, as with her father, she become a laudanum and opium addict and died before her time.

She married a cousin, Henry Nelson Coleridge, in 1829 and when he died in 1843 she continued what he was doing by editing her father's work – a father she was to see very seldom. In the meantime she wrote delightful verses for children, which were to become popular; her *Pretty Lessons in Verse for Good Children with some Lessons in Latin in Easy Rhyme* were originally written for her own children, although only two of her four children were to survive.

Her son Herbert Coleridge (1830–1861) won a double-first in classics and maths at Oxford and was secretary to a committee appointed by the Philological Society to work on the New English Dictionary. Her daughter Edith Coleridge was to finish writing her mother's autobiography and published it in 1873. Sara had started it for her daughter, who was nine when her mother died. Sara died of breast cancer, which, it was decided, was not wise to operate on. She described it as 'like the Ancient Mariner with the Albatross hung about his neck, I have a weight always upon me'.

Bradford Keyes Mudge, her biographer, described a period of her life from 1832 to 1833 as being her worst period when she:

> …gave herself up to opium and hysteria,
> throwing two 'fits' a day, sleeping only every
> third night and eating so little that her menstrual
> cycle stopped completely… From all accounts,
> her 'sad hysterical dejection' remained beyond
> the control of patient and doctors alike.

It would appear that the Coleridge manic-depressive illness had possibly been passed down to Coleridge's daughter, who had suffered from 'hideous' nightmares as a child – something it appears only her father understood and clearly sympathised with, as he insisted that a candle should henceforth be alight in her room when she retired to bed.

Vincent Van Gogh (1853–1890)

Who does not equate tortured creativity with the archetypal figure of Van Gogh and the tragic life story of the world's most famous but quintessentially troubled painter? He was an artist who will always be remembered for the torturous way that he famously suffered for his art, but who tragically never sold any of his work, only for his paintings to become the very epitome of collectable art globally after his death. His fantastic output of work comprised 1,000 drawings, 150 watercolours, ten watercolours, nine lithographs, and more than 900 paintings, all produced during his short decade of painting.

As the son of a pastor, he was brought up in a religious and cultured atmosphere. He was a highly emotional man, lacking in self-confidence, and struggled with his identity and direction. Initially he felt that his true vocation was to be a preacher and it took many years for him to discover himself as a painter. Before this discovery, he had experienced several unhappy relationships and taken jobs in bookshops, become a salesman and practised as a preacher in a poor area of Belgium where he was dismissed for being too zealous.

While his particular psychiatric diagnosis has been subject to much speculation since his suicide, it might appear to have been hereditary when you consider that his brother Theo also suffered from similar mood disorders, delusions and hallucinations, including violent behaviour, and was possibly even more melancholic than his brother. It was Theo who financed his brother's art career, being an important art dealer himself. He died six months after his brother, possibly because he was unable to cope with his brother's death.

In Van Gogh's case, his disorder eventually led him to painting, and much of his work can be seen as typical of someone suffering with manic depression: the over-vibrant colours of his pallette and the very harshness of his brush strokes speak of someone who was unable to hold back his emotions and needed to depict them with the most vivid of hues on canvas for all to see. His contoured forms were to significantly influence the Expressionist movement popular at the turn of the century in art. He frequently squeezed paint straight onto the canvas, being a spontaneous and instinctive painter, and worked at great speed to interpret what was feverishly going on in his head.

I can relate to the way he needed to paint, frequently, it seemed, being led by a particular muse that needed to be unravelled onto the canvas before he even knew what he was going to paint. I left an HNC course when they appeared to be instructing students to concentrate more on gathering notes prior to painting the subject. As with Van Gough, I find I paint better when I allow the mood to motivate me, and certainly not to order. I only wish I had been gifted with some of his talent.

It would appear to some that painting is a fun subject you can turn to for amusement or at will, but in my experience there's an underlying need compelling you to work at certain times and then, at others, the depths of your imagination have to be plumbed for inspiration.

When you embark on something that inspires you, there are likely to be more failures than successes. Even when a painting is finalised, an artist can only afford to feel pleased with his or her work briefly before they need to go on and make sure the next one is even better.

Van Gogh was finally incarcerated in a mental health hospital in Saint Rémy de Provence when he self-mutilated his ear after his disastrous relationship with Paul

Gauguin (himself another likely sufferer of the disorder). The two painters had been involved in a violent fight when working together in Arles in the south of France. Van Gogh continued to work intermittently on his paintings while in hospital suffering with alternate bouts of psychotic episodes and delusion, and his paintings during this time were seen to be more lyrical and alive: for instance, the painting of the cafe in Arles where the dark sky is alive with sinuous movement and wonder.

Van Gough, it is said, shot himself in despair over his financial reliance on his brother Theo and his inability to succeed with his art. After he shot himself he lived on for a few more days, saying, 'I hope I haven't botched it!' He insisted it was his right to do what he liked with his own body.

John Keats (1795–1821)

Keats, who has always been a favourite poet of mine, originally studied to be a surgeon. According to one of his fellow students, he spoke of little else than poetry when he was training and was heard to maintain that 'Poetry to my mind is the zenith of all my aspirations.' Keats clearly wanted to think of himself as a man of literature, also saying:

> Do you not see how necessary a World of
> Pains and troubles is to school an
> intelligence and make it a soul. A Place
> where the heart must feel and suffer in a
> thousand diverse ways.

Like others in his family, he was to die young of tuberculosis. It was nevertheless felt that many of his characteristics demonstrated that he was also likely to have suffered with manic depression. In his short lifetime he trained as a surgeon at Guy's Hospital in London before, with a handful of extraordinary poems, he received enough acclaim to became ranked alongside Shakespeare for his lyrical sonnets.

The family were reasonably prosperous and his mother was devoted to her children, particularly John. His father died of an accident when Keats was nine and his mother died four years later of tuberculosis, an illness that also took his brother Tom. When his grandmother eventually died, having taken on the task of bringing up the orphan family, Keats took on the responsibilities of his siblings.

When he fell in love with Fanny Brawne, he poured his affections into many of his most famous poems. They became engaged, but they never married because of his poor finances and ill health, and many of his later works show his dejection and his own deepest fears and frustrations about the situation at the time.

My favourite among his work is his last great poem, *To Autumn* – the ode being one of Keats' most iconic works and one in which he seems to have fully immersed himself in nature. Generations of readers still remember the first line, 'Season of mists and mellow fruitfulness', which always comes to my mind and sharpens my senses to the colours and the beauty of that particular season of the year. This was most especially so whenever I was in Canada in the fall and became the 'leaf peeper' in my area for the tourist board in Fredericton, reporting on the different stages of the vivid colours of the trees that surrounded my lakeside house.

The colours of the vast forest areas around me in the Maritimes can only be described as breath-taking, as though nature herself was experiencing a euphorically manic bipolar phase of her own. A certain person and a descendent of poets, when visiting me on the lake described me as 'Eve in Eden'.

Keats described himself as having a 'horrid morbidity of temperament', and he suffered from rapidly shifting moods. As a child he had been violent and ungovernable and was described by his brother as 'nervous and suffering from melancholy often followed by periods of intense activity and exhilaration'. It would appear to be the classic manic-depressive personality.

However, Keats had perhaps the most remarkable career of any English poet. Although he only published fifty-four poems, in three slim volumes as well as a few magazines, over his short lifetime he took on the challenges of a wide range of poetic forms from the sonnet to the romance, to the Miltonic epic, defining anew their possibilities with his own distinctive style. He is now seen as part of the British Romantic literary tradition, although he received no literary education.

Keats died of tuberculosis when he was twenty-five, having moved to Rome to live with a friend in the vain hope his health would improve while he was there.

The incidence of manic depression amongst other artists, writers and poets is staggeringly high. Among writers there were William Blake, Thomas Chatterton, Sylvia Plath, Virginia Woolf, Victor Hugo, Boris Pasternak and T.S. Eliot, all of whom were said to suffer with the disorder.

Composers include Edward Elgar, George Handel, Gustav Mahler, Sergei Rachmaninoff and Peter Tchaikovsky, and in the twentieth century Irving Berlin, Cole Porter and Noel Coward.

Among artists there were Richard Dadd, Paul Gauguin, Théodore Géricault, Arshile Gorky, Michaelangelo, Edvard Munch, Georgia O'Keeffe, Jackson Pollock, Dante Gabriel Rossetti and Mark Rothko.

T.S. Eliot, an important figure in twentieth-century literature, held the view that humans cannot bear to contemplate too much reality saying 'Grief and depression often bring with them for good or ill, the heart of life: the Inferno.' He quoted Plato's cave as being somewhere where all men have to face up to themselves.

Many of those listed also attempted suicide, although some, like me, did not succeed.

Virginia Woolf (1882–1941)

Virginia Woolf was an extraordinary English writer and an important modernist amongst twentieth-century writers. She also suffered emotionally with mood disorders and felt she was going mad before writing a final suicide note to her husband and drowning herself in the river. In her note she described how she felt she was going mad again and couldn't go through another episode, nor would she recover from it. She described how she was hearing voices which prevented her from concentrating, so this was the best thing to do. She says, 'You have given me the greatest possible happiness. You have been in every way all that anyone could be.' She felt that that no two people could have been happier except for this terrible disease. She ends the note with. 'I can't fight it any longer.'

Woolf was part of the famous Bloomsbury Set, which included her sister, Vanessa Bell, Leonard Woolf (her husband), Julia Margaret Cameron, her aunt and one of the greatest photographers of the age, Lytton Strachey and John Maynard Keynes, who were all to achieve fame during their lifetimes.

Her grandmother, mother and sister all suffered from bouts of depression, as well as her father and a brother. A cousin named James was institutionalised for manic depression and died of acute mania. She herself was frequently treated in hospital for psychotic manias and depression, finally committing suicide by weighing down her pockets with stones so she could drown herself.

She came from a large, creative family, who made regular commutes from their house in Kensington to Talland House on the rugged coast of Cornwall. These trips were to have influences on her later writings. She lost her mother in 1895 when she was thirteen, an event that presaged her eventual breakdown, especially after her stepsister died two years later and then her father died in 1904.

Her manic-depressive worries about her lack of talent as a writer as well as a woman, and her relationships with her husband and sister, overtook her and she attempted suicide in 1913. She was to sink into another depressed state that threatened her sanity two years later, but she was said to recover from this and keep it at bay until the end of her life.

These events alone would seem to be the hallmark of a bipolar sufferer. She had an affair with the painter Duncan Grant, who then went on to have an affair with her sister Vanessa. Angelica, their daughter, was born in 1918. Their unconventional and artistic home was to become a retreat for friends and relatives as well as many artists and writers of the day.

During her lifetime, however, she wrote far more fiction than many other famous writers, including Joyce and Faulkner. Six volumes of diaries, including early journals, six volumes of letters and numerous volumes of collected essays show her deep engagement with major twentieth-century issues. Many of her essays began as reviews written anonymously to improve her finances, and many include imaginative settings and thoughtful speculations, while they seriously question reading and writing, the arts, war and peace, politics and the need to reform society. She was also able to transform much of her dizzying heights of revelations to some of the most exquisite and sensitive lines in her poetry and writings. Her flights of euphoria revealed different understandings to her, which she found she could harness and add to her scintillating oeuvre.

Silvia Plath (1932–1963)

Like Virginia Woolf, Plath was a poet and a writer who spent her childhood in a comfortably well-off family, but she grew up over the pond in Boston in America. During her lifetime she attracted the attention of a multitude of readers, who empathised with her attempt to catalogue despair, violent emotion and a morbid obsession with death in her writings. Her poems explore her own intense emotions about her life, in particular her troubled marriage to English poet Ted Hughes, and her problems with her parents, as well as with her perception of herself. She is said to have stripped away the polite veneer of day-to-day life during the post-war period that so many women found so formidable.

She let her writing express elemental forces and primeval fears and by doing so, she laid bare the contradictions that tore apart appearances, hinting at some of the tensions hovering just beneath the surface of the American way of life during the post-war period. A former US poet laureate,

Robert Pinsky, wrote about her personality as 'being one who threw off images and phrases with the energy of a runaway horse, or an open-throttled machine.'

In a *New York Times* review it was said of Plath's early poems:

> Many of them offered themselves for
> sacrifice, transmuting agony, 'heart's waste,'
> into gestures and styles… She showed what
> self-absorption makes possible in art, and
> the price that must be paid for it, in the art as
> clearly as in the death.

In another newspaper review:

> At her most articulate, meditating on the
> nature of poetic inspiration, she is a
> controlled voice for cynicism, plainly
> delineating the boundaries of hope and
> reality. At her brutal best – she taps a source
> of power that transforms her poetic voice
> into a raving avenger of womanhood and
> innocence.

She was hospitalised for severe depression when she was twenty after attempting suicide by swallowing sleeping pills and received electric shock treatment. She ultimately succeeded in committing suicide at the age of 30 after her marriage had broken down and she was left with two young daughters, this time by turning on the gas taps. She described her anguish and depression after sleepless nights in her autobiography, *The Bell Jar*. It was her only published book.

The Bell Jar is a book I have been unable to read in full, as it obviously describes some of the feelings that I prefer not to revisit, although it lived on my bookshelf for a while. I sometimes feel rather too closely linked to parts of her story, especially the episodes when she was unable to sleep, some of which she described in the book as the feeling of sleeping with her eyes wide open whilst following the hands of her luminous bedside clock each night, every week without missing a second. She questioned whether she needed to wash each day, since it would only mean having to wash again the next.

She only saw her work *The Colossus* published in her lifetime, although she was a prolific poet. Hughes was to publish three other volumes of her poetry after her death, including *Ariel* and *Collected Poems* for which she was to win the 1982 Pulitzer Prize, posthumously.

Jackson Pollock (1912–1956)

Sometimes referred to as 'Jack the Dripper', owing to his idiosyncratic habit of crouching over a vast area of canvas while apparently looking as if he was casually splashing and besplattering his work with bright ribbons of colour, streaking across the air from his brush from different hues of brightly coloured household paint, Pollock was a leading exponent of what came to be called abstract expressionism. This is sometimes referred to as 'action painting' with its free association style of painting.

He became an influential American painter and a leading force behind the expressionist style of painting in the art world in the mid-twentieth century. During his lifetime, he was to enjoy considerable fame as well as notoriety, his major claim to fame being the creation and development of one of the most radical abstract styles in the history of modern art, by detaching line from colour, and finding original ways to describe space on vast canvases. This form of painting was said to have a direct relation to the artist's emotions, expression, and mood, and showcased the feeling behind the pieces they designed.

He was one of the first painters in America who was to achieve fame during his own lifetime. He was also a member of the Theosophical Society, a sect that promoted metaphysical and occult spirituality, although he had been brought up by his parents to be agnostic.

In 1937 he began psychiatric treatment for alcoholism leading to a nervous breakdown, after which he was hospitalised for four months. His paintings were used during his therapy treatment by two Jungian psychoanalysts, who encouraged Pollock to work from his unconscious. This was to encourage and eventually produce his unique and quintessential style.

Pollack's creative development of style particularly interests me as, when I started analytic therapy myself in my early forties, I was encouraged to paint in oils instead of the insipid watercolours I had become frustrated with. I found it such an inspirational and enthralling medium that I would become completely lost in it. When I then took along my paintings to my therapy sessions they would be carefully analysed by my therapist, Simon, as I'd had no idea at the time why I was painting strange pictures of empty faces and brightly coloured flora. It was grist to the mill and he soon enlightened me.

In 1943, Peggy Guggenheim promoted the new style of painting that Pollock was producing from his unconscious and held exhibitions in New York for him at her Art of This

Century gallery. The painter Lee Krassner, whom he married in 1945, was to stabilise his heavy drinking habits for a while and also handle his business affairs with Guggenheim.

Pollock died in a car accident in 1956 after his health had begun to deteriorate. It was thought to be suicide at the time but, to my thinking, if he became suicidal it was not only because he had a particular personality, one thought to be bipolar, but also due to the fact that his work had stagnated in a particular style that had become too rigidly his trademark. Thus he was unable to move on. In my experience, creativity, by its very nature, needs to continually spark something original in the mind of an artist in order to keep his or her impulses stimulated. Not only that, but it's vital for an artist to metamorphose onto the next level. A creative person can never afford to become too fixed in a style or overly content with his or her work overlong; their endeavours need to keep them constantly on the move, hence the restless spirit.

One of Pollock's sayings was:

> Today painters do not have to go to a matter
> outside of themselves. Most painters work
> from a different source. They work from
> within.

Perhaps he eventually found that going within was too painful a place to harvest. Nonetheless, in 2016, one of his paintings was reported to have fetched the extraordinary sum of $200 million in US dollars in a private purchase.

Present-day bipolar personalities

There are many personalities today who will willingly admit that their lives have been spectacularly altered due to their brushes with this disorder. Some have bravely and openly written about their struggles with it with a view to reducing its adverse reputation as a mental illness, while others appear to have been in its grip.

Stephen Fry

The heightened euphoric bouts of bipolar certainly have their price, particularly on the downward side of the disorder, when you sink into the proverbial abyss. Stephen Fry presumably experienced something of this when he left the West End play *Cell Mates,* in which he was starring, in the middle of its run and fled to Europe because he was experiencing the worst throes of his bipolar disorder. He talks about how he thought about ending his life, while sitting in a car with a blocked exhaust and considering whether to turn on the ignition. After returning from Europe he was diagnosed with the disorder at the age of thirty-seven. He said:

> For the first time I had a diagnosis that
> explained the massive highs and miserable
> lows I've lived with all my life.

In his 2006 documentary, *The Secret Life of a Manic Depressive,* he highlights his own experiences and the effects on him and other celebrities and members of the public. Fry presents this documentary by exploring the disease and portraying it as a still little understood, but potentially devastating condition affecting an estimated two per cent of the population. He embarks on an emotional journey to meet fellow sufferers to discuss the literal highs and lows of being bipolar. He maintains that of the 103 people who were interviewed with the condition, most would not push a button to remove it. However, despite Fry's views, apparently seventy-seven people out of the study, while reporting a wide variety of both positive and negative views of their condition, mostly wanted their disorder removed permanently.

Fry has also described how he would overspend his finances to a dangerous degree when in his manic phase, something I know I can sympathise with as I was also prone to enjoy overspending when 'high', believing at the time that all things were there for the asking and nothing was beyond my reach. Like Fry, I would never have wished to forego the exhilarating heightened awareness that this disorder affords you, the times when you feel entirely in tune with the world in your current enchanted orbit. For a while at least, you feel you are walking hand in hand with the gods. Who could forgo such an experience, however fleeting, and whatever the cost?

Tony Slattery

Fry's friend also admitted to the possibility that he was suffering from bipolar disorder when he appeared on a *Horizon* programme on TV. His regular appearances on *Whose Line is it Anyway?* as well as other comedy programmes made him a major star on the box in the nineties. But he has since battled with alcohol and drug problems that have kept him out of the public eye for many years. To quote from an interview he gave to *The Guardian* newspaper:

> Slattery seemed to be in a different world: a gifted actor and strikingly handsome, he vibrated with creativity and a barely suppressed inner darkness and you could never be sure how his skits would go but you knew they would have a jittery

brilliance to them, with a left-field lyrical twist or an emotional gut-punch. With his manic energy, he reminded me of Robin Williams, and it was clear that if he learned how to channel his talent there would be no stopping him… What happened to Slattery was not exciting, it was sad.

Robin Williams

The journal *Psychology Today*, although not a scholarly journal, is one that does have credible sources. When describing the illness Williams suffered from it states that he suffered from bipolar disorder with depression being part of its traits. The drugs and alcohol may have precipitated the end but manic-depression was the underlying problem.

His estranged wife has since added that depression was only one of his symptoms and the main one was a disease called Lewy body dementia.

Maria Carey

While it is said that one in four people suffer from some form of mental disorder, bipolar of late seems to have become something of a celebrity fetish, at least for some. Perhaps some of them imagine that tales of its exciting euphoric flights of fancy add further lustre to their star quality, but if they really knew the price that's extracted for such states, they might well think again.

That is certainly not to disparage in any way the personalities that have had the courage to speak out about being bipolar. The singer Maria Carey, who has maintained her position at the top of the music charts for many years, bravely disclosed in *People* magazine that until recently she had been in denial which made her vulnerable to people who might expose her. She found she couldn't carry the heavy burden any longer so sought treatment and found positive people to surround her so she could get back to writing songs and making music – the things that she loved.

Carey is now in therapy and taking medication for bipolar II disorder, which involves periods of depression as well as hypomania (less severe than the mania associated with bipolar I disorder, but one that can still cause irritability, sleeplessness and hyperactivity). She says she freely admits she was irritable and 'in constant fear of letting people down.' She says she eventually 'hit a wall', and describes how lonely and guilty she felt because she wasn't able to do what she needed to do to boost her career.

She says she is now in a good place where she is comfortable discussing her struggles with bipolar II disorder. She says she is hopeful that a place can be reached where such a disorder is no longer stigmatised so people no longer have to struggle with it alone. It's a disorder which is incredibly isolating but it doesn't have to define or control you.

Carrie Fisher (1956-2016)

The much-loved star of Hollywood, who first came to prominence when playing Princess Leia in *Star Wars*, has been described online as 'the ultimate hero for people with mental illness'. However, her most feminist act was her frankness about being bipolar because she believes that women who show signs of this are usually defined as 'crazy'.

An online article states that Fisher was first diagnosed with the disorder when she was twenty-nine, after a drug overdose that nearly killed her. She wasn't alone, as around sixty per cent of people with bipolar have abused drugs or alcohol at some point, often because they're instinctively attempting to stabilise their mood swings. She's quoted as saying that, at the time, 'drugs made me feel more normal… They contained me.' At the peak of her addiction she was taking thirty Percodan (a narcotic medicine) a day. When doctors told her she had a treatable illness underneath the drug problem, she refused to believe it. 'I thought they told me I was manic depressive to make me feel better about being a drug addict.'

After a release from rehab, Fisher immediately threw a huge party, featuring a rented ambulance and a cardboard cut-out of Princess Leia strapped to a gurney (stretcher) with an IV (intravenous needle) in her arm.

Along with her other self-disparaging and highly amusing books, which I thoroughly enjoyed reading, her novel *Postcards from the Edge* was made into a film, with Meryl Streep playing Fisher and Shirley MacLaine playing her mother, the film star Debbie Reynolds. A semi-autobiography, it's filmed as a comedy/drama story of a fallen Hollywood actress not only struggling to get back from alcoholism but who is also trying to emerge from the shadow of her famous film-star mother.

Talking about mental illness in such a frank way was a brave act, particularly for a woman who admitted to being sensitive to media criticism, said Sandy Doyle in a *Quartz* business media article. Further adding;

> To be a woman is to live with the perpetual
> threat of being called crazy. But to be a
> woman with actual mental illness is
> something else again. No matter who you are,
> no matter what you do, the world treats you as
> a worst case scenario and a dirty joke,
> someone who has failed at being female.

Fisher was open about the fact that it was her story, in part to defuse the uglier, crueller stories that surfaced regardless. 'Things come out in the media about me. When it's out there, it's someone else's version of me. I want it to be my version,' she said.

She was also instrumental in the launching of *BP Magazine* in 2004 and appeared on three of its covers. She said:

> One of the things that baffles me…is how there
> can be so much lingering stigma with regards to
> mental illness, specifically bipolar disorder. In
> my opinion living with manic depression takes
> a tremendous amount of balls.

She also made the point that, 'Bipolar disorder can be a great teacher. It's a challenge but it can set you up to be able to do almost anything else in your life.'

I can certainly vouch that once you have descended to the depths of your soul and experienced the abyss, there is nothing else in life that could scare you as much.

After a successful career in films, especially her role in the *Star Wars* series, Carrie Fisher had a turbulent personal life. After surviving her parents' very public divorce, and several divorces and difficult relationships of her own, she was to die of a sudden cardiac arrest at the age of sixty, after experiencing a medical emergency during a transatlantic flight from London to Los Angeles. Her daughter announced that, 'She battled drug addiction and mental illness her entire life. She ultimately died of it.'

Like myself, she had a stormy relationship with her mother, in her case Debbie Reynolds, but they were close at the end and her mother died of a stroke the day after her daughter, apparently saying, 'I want to be with Carrie.'

Mel Gibson

It's not just 'crazy ladies' that suffer from this unpredictable and beguiling disorder and who come in for media speculation. A certain Mel Gibson of movie fame has also displayed some fairly 'crazy' behaviour, like the time he made headlines after he launched an anti-Semitic tirade toward a police officer who was arresting him on a charge of drunken driving.

This was followed by the time when two audiotapes were leaked of him purportedly threatening his ex-girlfriend, the mother of one of his nine children. She later reported that he was physically abusive. The messy headlines ended his star power and made him virtually un-hireable, but then he bounced back. Gibson finally admitted in a documentary in 2008 that he had been diagnosed with bipolar disorder and some of his aggressive behaviour could be consistent with a person suffering with that kind of problem.

Gibson has managed to survive despite insulting and denigrating gay, Black and Jewish people at different times, and although his career has been riddled with accusations of racism and domestic violence, it's something that has been put down to his alcoholism.

He now appears to have got his life under control and is planning and appearing in films again, with directors saying he is a changed person and one who is well liked and professional when working on a set.

A psychiatrist called Douglas Bey Jr, who wrote a book titled *Loving a Depressed Man*, stated that being irritable is a prime symptom of bipolar, especially if someone was not medicating to stabilise their mood.

Non-compliance with medication is a common problem among bipolar patients. One of the worst complications with this disorder is the way sufferers are in denial of their mental condition, and, as Bey points out, when they are on a high or during a manic phase, those in creative fields like Mel Gibson, can feel that their medication is going to seriously slow them down when they are at the top of their game.

Vivien Leigh (1913–1967)

Leigh started performing when she was three, singing a nursery rhyme in her mother's amateur theatre group. Later, in 1936, she fell in love with Laurence Olivier when they were both married to other partners, from whom they were subsequently divorced. When Olivier left her to go abroad to play Heathcliff in *Wuthering Heights*, she began to show signs of her lifetime mental illness. There was no treatment for the disorder at the time, so it went undiagnosed and, over time, she became ever more difficult to work with on the sets of the films in which she was contracted to play. Having been born in India, it's possible she also contracted tuberculosis when she was a child – another illness that can become a lifetime ailment.

Olivier used his contacts to get her the much-coveted role of Scarlett O'Hara in the upcoming film *Gone with the Wind,* which was to win her an Oscar and make her name. After they married, the couple were to go on and star in many films together, although staging *Romeo and Juliet* on Broadway in New York was thought to be in somewhat bad taste considering their recent divorces. In the end it was considered a flop – such were the mores of the day.

Leigh then suffered a miscarriage, possibly from the tuberculosis illness still in her system, as well as experiencing frequent bipolar mood swings involving several days of hyperactivity followed by a deep depression and a breakdown consisting of 'shivering fits and swear-filled tirades,' according to *The Hollywood Reporter.*

She saw her husband knighted for his roles, which had caused his success to soar above hers, and, although she valiantly kept on working, the marriage was doomed to failure, as Olivier eventually found it too hard to keep up with her extreme mood swings and frequent outbursts and she had admitted to an affair with Peter Finch. When she appeared in *A Streetcar Named Desire,* playing the role of an emotionally unstable Blanche DuBois, she admitted later that the part 'tipped me over into madness'.

She worked successfully to the end of her life, although at times she was very obviously unwell. She married again after her divorce from Olivier and suffered yet another miscarriage. She died of tuberculosis in 1967, and Olivier had continued to show concern towards her and had kept in touch until the end.

In her obvious desire to overcome her bipolar illness, Leigh, who was not only beautiful but gifted enough to appear on the world stage, managed to remain successful until the end, working tirelessly in a profession she had presumably found to somewhat assuage her demons. With bipolar you are apt to throw everything you have into whatever creative endeavour you find that can suitably sustain your desire to excel.

Among a few other famous names who have admitted to being bipolar are Frank Sinatra, Francis Ford Coppola, Buzz Aldrin, Jim Carey, Irving Berlin, and, of course, Amy Winehouse.

Amy Winehouse (1983–2011)

Winehouse was an extremely talented singer-songwriter who indulged in substance abuse, no doubt as a result of her underlying bipolar disorder. It was something she admitted to in several interviews around the time of the release of the album that included the song *Rehab,* a clear expression of some of her anguish: 'It's not just my pride/it's just 'til these tears have dried.'

The bipolar disorder she suffered from, which shadowed her life, eventually killed her. She was not known to have sought treatment for the disorder, although she admitted to having problems with self-harm, depression and eating disorders. She also said she was manic depressive and not an alcoholic, although she added that it sounded like an 'alcoholic in denial'.

She started a tumultuous on-off relationship with music video assistant Blake Fielder-Civil, whom she later married and who admitted to introducing her to hard drugs. In public, the couple's arguments and fist-fights spilled out across the media, with their dramatic scenes appearing in the red-top newspapers. Amy was hospitalised in 2007 after she admitted she had overdosed with a mixture of booze and hard drugs and had to put on hold her planned tour of North America.

Her most famous album, *Back to Black,* earned her many musical awards and plaudits and her recording became a number one in January 2007, selling 1.85 million copies over the course of the year. One music writer, when praising Winehouse for her confidence, also added, 'What she is, is mouthy, funny, sultry, and quite possibly mad.'

Dr David Sack of Promises Addiction Treatment Centre in Los Angeles, described how she minimised the extent to which her life was dominated by drugs and alchohol and the extent to which her addictions were effecting her. As he saw it, most of those who are drug dependent are frightened to seek treatment and drugs get glamorised in the entertainment community where it becomes the acceptable norm.

Like Vivian Leigh with her acting, Winehouse was to have frequent breaks from her singing career when the pressure of the music scene became too much for her. She was booed off the stage at a Hammersmith concert, with fans saying that she looked 'highly intoxicated throughout'. At the time, she said her doctor had advised her to take a complete rest.

During her fourteen years of active work, she restlessly travelled the globe to sing at international concerts while tirelessly working on new recordings with writers to add to her albums.

Amy, who became an icon for youth culture with her deep, expressive contralto voice, was just twenty-seven years of age when she died of alcohol intoxication in July 2011.

One US reporter wrote that Winehouse was a 'victim of mental illness in a society that doesn't understand or respond to mental illness with great effectiveness'. I think, for me, that particular summing up says it all, not only for Winehouse but for many others who suffer with this mental disorder's quixotic demands.

Catherine Zeta Jones

When Zeta Jones checked into a clinic in 2011 for five days because she said she suffered from bipolar disorder, she was highly praised by mental health charities, who said her disclosure would have a huge impact. The charities congratulated her on her courage in speaking up and even the red-top tabloids treated her with dignity. An article in *The Guardian* stated: 'No amount of PR spend could have brought Catherine Zeta Jones the fund of sympathy and goodwill she has received after announcing she was being treated for bipolar disorder.'

Zeta Jones starred in a number of TV comedy series, most famously *The Darling Buds of May*, before moving to Hollywood, gaining a best supporting actress Oscar in the all-singing, all-dancing *Chicago*, then going on to marry a major film star, Michael Douglas, 25 years her senior. She has two children with Douglas.

Many problems have befallen her, including being sent threatening letters by a woman who was infatuated with her husband. Her husband suffered with stage IV throat cancer and the initial news of Douglas's diagnosis was something she is said to have found particularly difficult to cope with and was the trigger for her decision to check into a mental health facility for a brief stay to treat her bipolar II disorder.

In *The Guardian* article, Marjorie Wallace, chief executive of the mental health charity Sane, is quoted as saying:

Zeta Jones' announcement will have a huge
impact on other people recognising mental
illness is a condition that everyone can
suffer from. The importance is for people to
accept it's a treatable illness rather than one
they have to live with for years so that they
become more and more sucked into a
downward spiral and at risk of suicide.

In the same article, *The Guardian* notes that bipolar disorder is estimated to affect up to 2.4 million people in the UK and sufferers are estimated to be ten times more likely to kill themselves than the rest of the population. The average time for seeking help, it says, is after four to five years and a US survey showed that it took an average of 10.2 years for a correct diagnosis and treatment. Although bipolar disorder is often first experienced in the teens or twenties, any extra trauma can often tip sufferers into a crisis.

Stephen Fry, Alastair Campbell and Ruby Wax have also all spoken publicly about their experiences with bipolar in the press and on TV. Their aim, it seems, is to make this disorder one that is more easily recognised and lift the stigma from those who suffer from its more negative aspects.

Ruby Wax

In an article in *The Guardian* in 2011, Ruby Wax said, 'I think I became a cartoon to escape how ill I was.' The lively and uncompromising comedian has studied neuroscience at Oxford University in order to become a psychotherapist, something she had originally started to study at Berkeley University in California before she dropped out. Wax has had several spells at The Priory hospital in Roehampton, West London, in an attempt to come to terms with her disorder. She has also admitted to spending an inordinate amount of time searching for the right medication that works for her particular type of the disorder.

She also introduced me to the word 'anhedonia', which she mentioned she was suffering from at one time. It means an inability to feel pleasure in anything you usually find enjoyable. The word describes a feature that is a common symptom of depression as well as other mental health disorders, like bipolar and schizophrenia. Most people understand what pleasure feels like and expect certain things in life to normally make them happy, but people who experience anhedonia have lost interest in the activities they normally enjoy. It's a core symptom of major depressive disorder, although it can also be a symptom of other mental health problems.

Since gaining her masters from Oxford for mindfulness based on cognitive therapy, as well as an OBE for her services to mental health, Wax has created stage shows and written bestselling books on the subject of mental health. With her talents as a comedian, she has been able to put a different slant on a subject that many people find hard to verbalise. With her quirky and original sense of humour, she has been able to make light of a subject that many people fear, as well as find hard to get their head around.

In March 2017 she launched Frazzled Cafe in partnership with Marks & Spencer. These are cafes where you can go and find others when they feel 'frazzled'. In 2007 she was also announced as the president of Relate, the UK's leading relationship-supporting charity.

When she embarked on her book, *A Mindfulness Guide for the Frazzled,* she says, 'I was trying to find out what was wrong with me.' She has suggested instead of asking people, 'How are you?' when you meet, 'try to go below the radar and ask them to divulge more, by asking about the weather conditions in their head; in an effort to attempt to get them to open up on the subject'.

Wax has lately become a keen advocate for mindfulness, describing it online as something that isn't just about marinating in your own thoughts and being self-obsessed. She sees it as becoming aware of your internal state so you don't dump it on those around you and then blame them for your own unhappiness.

She is also an Aries, like me, and currently lives mostly alone in her one-up, one-down 'nano' house in the country, happy to be away from the spotlight while practising her meditation and writing.

Kim Novak

In a recent interview in *The Guardian*, Novak admitted that when she was in Hollywood making films like *Vertigo* with James Stewart and *Pal Joey* with Frank Sinatra she realised she was 'too fragile for fame' and she now works as a mental health activist.

She said that working in Hollywood you can get lured into loving yourself too much and that's why she left because, she said, 'She didn't want to lose herself.' In other words, she felt she needed to leave to save herself. She said she likes who she is even with the suffering you go through and the fact that, when you're vulnerable, you feel everything so intensely. She asserts that she inherited her mental illness through her father, and that she never wanted children herself as she didn't want to pass down her inheritance to them. Her other love is art and she has published a book of her work, which portrays animals as well as abstracts. She never turned to drugs or alcohol as, she says, 'Painting has always been there to rescue me.'

As with myself, Novak didn't recognise her bipolar until she was diagnosed with it when she was nearly seventy. Since then she has spent time trying to normalise it, telling people it's just another illness that can be treated (in her case with antipsychotics) and not one to be stigmatised. She says she didn't like lithium because it made her put on weight, but that her art has had a positive effect on her bipolar and vice versa. 'All those rages and feelings of depression, they leave you when you let them out. And that's what painting is all about.' Her husband of 45 years recently died and she asserts, 'Painting got me though it.'

Dame Rachel Whiteread

In a recent article in *The Guardian*, the famous artist revealed how a diagnosis of bipolar had changed her work, saying, 'I have a clarity I never had before.' She had made two major works (now on view in London) that weren't her usual enormous, rough casts reflecting the appalling crises going on in the world, which have affected her so deeply in the past. After thirty-five years of working as a sculptress, she has completely changed her language, or rather, as she says, 'expanded my vocabulary'.

Whiteread was diagnosed with bipolar at the age of fifty, and has been hospitalised a few times. However, the diagnosis, she says, 'Has made me realise I have always been an 'emotional sponge – a thing can happen and you sort of unravel.' She reveals that she would not have felt comfortable talking about the condition in the past but feels it's a good thing for people to know that successful people can also be very ill. Her new works are part of her reaching an accommodation with the diagnosis, even harnessing it. She says in *The Guardian* article:

> I am now able to take a step back and say, I
> know what's going on. And not
> compartmentalise it, but to understand and

use it in some way. It's fed into my
creatively. In a way which I think is clear.

Whiteread was the first women to win the annual Turner Prize in 1993. She was also one of the YBAs (Young British Artists) who exhibited at the Royal Academy's Sensation exhibition in 1997.

It's true that there is going to be information available about people who are in the public eye. As Anthony Storr recollected in his *The Sanity of True Genius,* the more we learn about other people the easier it is for us to pick up what we see as their neurotic traits. From now on the famous and successful will find it more difficult to hide whatever failings they possess as their biographers and PhD students are unlikely to leave them in peace.

Proust is said to have alleged, 'everything great comes from neurotics. They alone have founded religions and composed our masterpieces,' while Seneca, who was forced to commit suicide in 65AD, succinctly remarked, 'There has never been great talent without some admixture of madness.' John Dryden, the poet and literary critic, likewise agreed: 'Great wits are sure to madness near allied. And thin partitions do their bounds divide.' However, it should be pointed out that not all creative geniuses are necessarily suffering from a disorder. Peter Paul Rubens was a hard-working and hugely wealthy individual who was not only employed by the Duke of Mantua but also by the Infanta Isabella, in the face of personal bereavement, to be a diplomat. In 1624 he was granted a patent of nobility by Isabella's nephew Philip IV and in 1627 she moved him even further up the social scale by making him a 'gentleman of the household'. As Dr Storr points out, 'No one could be further removed from the notion that artists are necessarily tormented beings.'

There was also Hans Holbein the Younger, born in 1497, who was to paint 150 court portraits for Henry VIII. The Tudor monarch brought him over from Germany to be a court painter, as he was thought to be the most exquisite draftsman of all time. Holbein carefully kept himself apart from political authority that might inhibit his creative powers but the king thought well enough of his diplomatic skills to send him to the Continent to help select a bride for him, having absolute confidence in his wise choice.

Many people with a particular genius, alongside bipolar inclinations, appear to avoid forming close relationships in their lives, perhaps forming distant bonds or short liaisons instead. Many find it necessary to keep people at a distance so they can find the space to develop their thinking as well as play with certain concepts in their minds and not be open to thoughtless derision or to other people's ideas. Their emotional isolation from others gives them space and time to work with their epigrammatic ideas. Some others just find it easier to be alone with their thoughts than grappling with other's idiosyncrasies.

Joe Griffin and Ivan Tyrrell, who originated the methodology 'Human Givens', have made reference in their book *Godhead* to autism being left-brain thinking and conversely bipolar being right-brain thinking. They also assert that when our brains made the giant leap from REM dreaming at night to daytime dreaming, thereby producing innovation and original thought – which they describe as a 'Big Bang' in our brain's evolution – this was the astounding mind-enhancing occurrence that was to allow us to begin to think creatively. 'Autism and schizophrenia are related,' they insist, and from that time forwards, each one of us has had the chance to be effective from the fallout that unlocked imagination and reason when this occurred some 40,000 years ago. They suggest that from then on the human race was forever changed being one that could access the REM state by balancing right brain abilities with the strengths of the left brain hemisphere, allowing them to maintain stability.

They link this to the appearance around that time of early works of art such as carvings, sculptures, drawings and cave paintings.

As for myself, I'd feel an overwhelming sadness when depressed and sometimes used to get the feeling that I'd never see my adult sons again when they said goodbye to me at the end of a visit. But I learned that the work you do when recovering from depression is more vitally meaningful, since you are now returning to life with more knowledge about yourself as well as your creativity, which has travelled to the surface with you from deep in your unconscious. Could this be where the idea comes from that you quintessentially have to suffer for your art – and by doing so are subsequently branded as mad or even bad when you become impatient and bad tempered if your fevered train of thought is interrupted? Your mind is desperately trying to bring your nascent ideas to the surface and thereby bring them to fruition in whichever way you wish to creatively convey them; it becomes of vital importance to grasp them before they fade away again.

However, perhaps this could answer some questions as to why so many manic-depressive people are creatively empowered. During their depressive state they have not only plumbed the depths of their storehouse, where creativity is housed in the unconscious, but when they are in recovery and soaring back into blue sky territory, they heroically want to share their lofty ideas with others. This personifies the myth of Persephone, who was said to bring back the spring when she emerged from her ordeal in the Underworld with Hades, allowing flowers to bloom and trees to blossom once again.

It is the creativity aspect that makes bipolar so difficult to treat, as many sufferers would not be willing to give up their periods of artistry and submit to being subdued into a state of languid somnambulism. They've paid dearly with their incarceration in the void and they are certainly not going to lose one iota of that precious scintilla of creativity they are now emerging with by dulling it with some chemical medication.

Chapter 5

DIAGNOSING AND TREATING BIPOLAR

One of the most difficult problems with bipolar is the lack of insight when it comes to recognising the disorder in yourself. It is so easy to be in self-denial about bipolar and not seek a diagnosis, even when your actions might land you in hospital. I made up my mind I was never going to allow anyone to put me on long-term drugs like my mother and sister, both of whom have suffered with depression.

As a result, it would be many years until I personally reached some kind of self-realisation and admitted to being bipolar. We know now that if this disorder is not diagnosed in childhood it can be particularly dangerous in adulthood but, of course, when I was young it was not something that anyone talked about, especially not if it was hidden away in the dark cupboards of the family history, with people feeling it would be a stain on their standing in society should word get out. Not only that, but it wasn't even understood enough at that time for it to be clinically diagnosed.

I spent years trying to do the work on myself with various therapists, analysts and counsellors before I finally came to the important conclusion that I suffered from bipolar. My first analyst, Dr Snow, managed to get me out my coercive marriage but left me with the toxic idea that I was self-destructive, which was to leave me with years of underlying fears that would surface whenever I was in a depressive state and believed I might harm myself. It also had a detrimental effect on my relationship with my two sons. The ripples that emanated from this diagnosis were pervasive and had a long-term damaging effect on my life.

I remember one day finding myself alone in the house and having a panic attack, morosely considering the fact that my sons would soon be adult enough to leave home. When I phoned Dr Snow in desperation, he showed an evident lack of interest in my state, coldly telling me, 'Call an ambulance.'

And so my journey to diagnosis with bipolar was a long one. I was to return to Canada for another visit five years after my partner Robert died, and during my millennium-year tour of America in 2000, I once again traversed the US continent after flying to see my cousin Prudence in Idaho. I then travelled with her on a trip to Cascade, driving there along the mighty Sawtooth mountain range via Sun Valley. Here we stayed in a log cabin in the woods, which brought back evocative memories of my life with Robert in the Maritimes. From Sun Valley I travelled on to San Francisco to stay with Ann, the friend of a friend who had kindly agreed to put me up in her elegantly tall Ashbury Heights house overlooking the iconic Golden Gate Bridge. Although we had never met, when I arrived she was baking a chocolate cake to welcome me.

Flying back to New York, I ended my tour when I drove myself back up to New Brunswick in Canada once more. After waking up in a log home in an Idaho forest with trees and wildlife around me, I was now even more keen to find another place on a lake in the Maritimes to continue my painting aspirations. I wasn't interested in recreating my life with Robert now he was gone; I needed to find somewhere that I could renovate myself this time, and where I could continue my painting. I returned the following year, determined to find my perfect property and location where I would have the space to work on large canvases again.

By then much had happened. My father had died, aged ninety-one, in 1997, and my mother, having found it difficult on her own, had been taken into hospital when she attempted to take her life with an overdose. It seemed to be a tradition in the family – since all three daughters had, at one time or another, made nihilistic but fortunately unsuccessful suicide attempts. The fact that she had asked me to go and live with her only indicated how low she must have been feeling. Living together with my mother would, I'm sure, have proved a disaster – we had never been able to get on for long. However, her last words to me were very much a surprise when she said, 'I just want you to know how very, very important you are to me and how much I love you.' It seemed very sad that she hadn't been able to share those words with me before her life was all but at an end.

When I visited my mother in an upbeat mood, she'd often try her best to undermine me by making malicious comments about the people I cared about, such as my beloved godmother, my Aunt Marion, or my two sisters, knowing I'd immediately defend them. Being bipolar means your emotions are near to the surface and she was well aware of how to wind me up – as I was equally aware of her motives. On one occasion, when I got up to leave the house before I lost my cool, when I crossed the room in mid-flow, she reached out and theatrically struck me on the arm. When, in mocking fashion, I stopped and returned her gesture, she spread a rumour around the family that I had gone to her house and assaulted her.

I had by then moved to the West Country near Bath, to the unique and historic town of Bradford-on-Avon, having sold my London home. I bought a cottage on a hillside, which overlooked a valley and the famous White Horse at Westbury, to begin my long-desired Foundation art course at Bath College.

The following year, I once again booked a late spring flight to Halifax, Nova Scotia, hiring a car and finally completing my tour of Cape Breton before driving back to Fredericton in the Maritimes to seriously look for a lakeside property. In New Brunswick, most lake properties – or cottages as they call them – get passed down through families, but I was lucky enough to find one that was being sold because the couple who had been living there had decided to separate.

It was about thirty-five miles east along the St John River from Fredericton and a perfect site for me, a little way down a track that wove its winding way between majestic tall fir trees. When we reached the property and I looked down through the leafy tree-lined driveway at the side of the house, I spied an idyllic sparkling lake glistening in the distance. I had found my reverie – one that seemed to me to be the personification of my dreams.

It was a two-storey, dove-grey, weather-boarded dwelling with three small balcony bedrooms up top and glass sliding doors opening from a large living room onto a wide deck that encompassed the entire front of the house. From here, steps led down to the garden, which had a pathway through it to the shore of the lake. Of course, it needed work to make it winterproof, as the water tank was precariously positioned outside. The kitchen also needed renovating and a studio room built across the far side, with another bedroom above it. I managed to raise a mortgage to buy it, but during my first year there I was not yet in a position to pay for builders to carry out the renovations.

Thus I spent that first summer in my lakeside house, enjoying the wonderful weather and getting myself used to the hordes of early springtime mosquitoes that were furiously thirsting after my blood, even managing to bite me through the canvas of the hammock I erected between the trees. Here I could swing gently as I gazed across a wide stretch of peaceful lake. Fortunately, the mozzies were toast once the dragonflies came and had them for breakfast by conveniently hoovering them up. Then came the infinitely more welcome hummingbirds looking for the sugar water that I hung above my balcony for them so I could watch them, their iridescent wings moving nineteen to the dozen like a honeybee, while they aggressively fought off any similar bird that might dare to come near. There was a family of bright blue jays that visited the many seed baskets I erected and cute little chipmunks that scuttled around below my deck. Ospreys, golden eagles and the loons were also part of the engaging scene, as were the red squirrels that managed to outwit every effort I made to stop them stealing the birdseed.

On my next return to the UK, it was clear that my mother was nearing the end. The unfortunate confusion she'd further stirred up between myself and my sisters when she asked me to take over the power of attorney responsibilities (which my youngest sister had already assumed) brought even more family problems to a head, orchestrating the end of any future hopes I might have had of ever achieving a sustainable relationship with either of them. It was something that was already a fragile scenario. I couldn't wait to get back to the lake to start putting my new building plans into action.

My mother died that summer of 2001 and the money from her estate enabled me to pay off my lakeside mortgage as well as take a trip to see my elder son Leon in Thailand to celebrate Christmas with him and Nicky, who had been enjoying a yoga holiday in India and came to join us. It was the first time we had all enjoyed such an exotic Christmas Day, with a full celebration lunch on the beach and a swim afterwards in the cool blue of the hotel's large outside pool. It was, for once, a peaceful family Christmas and one to remember.

On New Year's Day, however, I realised my son Nicky was far from well when he visited me in the hotel I'd booked on Koh Samui to watch the colourful firework display from my beachside room. When he left to catch his flight home, I sent a message to his father, Mike, to ask him to make sure he saw a doctor on his return, although I don't believe anything was ever done about it. Nicky was now in his thirties so there was little more I could do.

The following year was spent renovating my lakeside home, unfortunately at first with a bogus builder who had to be sent on his way *tout suite*. The following year I hired Doug, who had to almost rebuild what had been done by someone I'd naively trusted but who'd duped me into believing he had some skills. But then I was only just beginning to learn about Canadian builders.

While I was in Thailand, I'd met an American who appeared to be constantly travelling the globe, *Flying Dutchman* style. When I suggested meeting up again and visiting Nepal, a place I was keen to see, he seemed to baulk a little at the idea and consequently put me in touch with a British friend he'd made while abroad. He turned out to be related to two of the most famous English poets of the nineteenth century, since his parents had finally reunited the two esteemed families with their prestigious marriage.

After a year of painstaking rebuilding, during which I remained on the lake throughout the cold winter months with snow drifts up to my knees and frozen indoor plumbing, by the beginning of the summer of 2003 I had a beautifully renovated house. As well as a large studio on the side for my work, I had a stunning galleried bedroom above with a pitched wooden ceiling and a skylight window through which I could gaze upwards to the stars at night and wake to views across the peaceful lake.

I was ready to receive my first visitor, the man who bore the same name of a famous poet and who arrived from London to stay. It was to be the start of an interesting but sometimes rather fraught eight-year relationship, and another one played out between two continents.

During his first month with me, we travelled the length and breadth of New Brunswick and went whale watching in Nova Scotia, travelling as far afield as Bar Harbour in Maine and down to Boston in Massachusetts. I would then enjoy having somewhere to stay in London with him in his flat in Chelsea whenever my plane touched down in London. Two houses in two continents and a glamorous boyfriend to stay with in town – what was not to like? Throughout the first two years I knew Silas (his pseudonym), we would keep in touch every day by phone, text or email – sometimes all three – until I discovered he was playing a double game. From then on I damped down on the daily communications and decided two can play at that game. After all – hadn't I decided long ago I was never going to remarry or share my life with anyone again?

By 2004 my new life of commuting between two continents was up and running and I was teaching an art course at the local university; running portrait workshops, as well as spending time at the Beaverbrook Gallery, where I had been invited to become one of their docents. It was a role that included attending fascinating weekly meetings where we would be introduced to the next artist to exhibit at the gallery in order to understand their work and explain it to the public when they visited. We would also be taken on interesting trips to art galleries throughout

New England, where we met with other gallery docents and were given tours of their exhibits.

Meantime, I was enjoying painting in my new up-and-running studio and had arranged an exhibition in nearby Oromocto, near to the Davis family, who had been close friends of Robert and had now become my surrogate Canadian family with their four delightful children.

I was still meeting up with Martin from time to time, when he would treat me to an English breakfast downtown. He had also visited me at my now completed lakeside house, but although he seemed keen to continue our relationship as before, I was determined to keep it as a friendship. I had also started to see a writer, Wayne, who I become fond of and who bought one of my sunflower paintings, telling me that he had it hanging in a prominent place, 'where I can enjoy seeing it.' After a party at his brother's house one evening we visited his summer log house northwards, on the banks of the mighty Miramichi River, famous with the Americans for its salmon fishing holidays. We would continue to meet up in town and still keep in touch online. He went on to publish twenty books and gain popularity, winning numerous awards for his books, articles and poetry.

Since his father's death, it was now obvious that Nicky was becoming unstable and, while I had always worried that Leon would find his life the more challenging with his massive intellect but frail disposition, it came as a shock to me that Nicky was failing too and was possibly in an even more precarious position than his older brother.

Leon was still living in Thailand and the next winter I decided to go and visit him for the second time and this time take my grandson with me to see his father. It was the winter of 2004 and when the time came for me to drive to London to spend the Christmas holiday with Nicky in his flat in town, we were all in for a huge shock, as on Boxing Day the news filtered through that there had been a giant tsunami disaster in the area.

After many family discussions, my grandson Jake finally decided that we should go. As we hadn't heard anything, I especially needed to make sure Leon was safe. Jake and I at last arrived on the island of Koh Samui off the Thai peninsular, en route for Koh Phenang and Leon; we were late, as most of the planes had been diverted to the disaster area. It was a huge shock when he wasn't there to meet us, but Leon had already gone back to his own island, thinking we wouldn't be coming.

Fortunately, we finally contacted him and, after a night in a luxury hotel and a refreshing midnight swim in their pool, we were reunited with my son on his island the next day, when he came to meet us at the ferry.

My house in the UK had been let for a year and, on my return from Thailand, I had booked a flat in an art studio complex in Cheriton on the Gower peninsular in south Wales. I had two disconcerting visitors while I was there. Silas came to see me first and was his usual insouciant and obfuscating self, annoying me to such a point that shortly after he left I became so lost in thought one morning when pondering how to end the vexing relationship that I blindly stepped out onto a road and into the path of an oncoming car. My foot and elbow were injured in the process. When I left hospital, I was given codeine tablets for the pain, but they obviously didn't agree with me as, when I got up in the night feeling nauseous, I knocked myself out when I collapsed on the bedpost – necessitating further medical help at the hospital early the next morning.

Staying on the tip of the Gower peninsular, I now found myself miles from anywhere and I couldn't even drive, so I asked Nicky to come and stay and drive me back to

Bradford where I could rent a flat for a month until I was due to go back to Canada. When he arrived he seemed distant and distracted, and when we got back to the flat in Bradford he stayed for a few days, behaving in a strange and uncharacteristic way, having seemingly got the idea that he and his brother had been regularly groomed from birth for some higher grandiose plan. I'm now aware that this is a typical symptom of a bipolar disorder manic phase, but because he was so entirely convincing, it was a disturbing notion to Leon and me at the time.

When I finally got back to Canada early in 2005, having rented out the house there during that winter, I finally got back to my life and enjoying my painting as well as spending time at the Beaverbrook Gallery. However, things slowly continued to disintegrate and it was abysmally turning into a proverbial 'annus horribilis' for me.

The spring in Canada that year was a washout and many of the cottages on the lake flooded, as Indian lake, where I lived, was subject to the tides. I spent many days watching from my deck while nervously willing the lake to recede and not enter my house. Also, by then I had realised that the 9/11 event in New York, which I had watched on TV on a trip into town in 2001, had disastrously affected my shares and nearly half of my investments had now been eroded.

But worse than that was the news from London that Nicky had lost another job and was drifting dangerously. Although I had found a therapist for him to see, he had long ago given up his appointments with him. The realisation that he was obviously so ill he now needed to be hospitalised was so distressing that it cast me back into a deep depression and, although it was now past the height of summer, when everyone was packing up their lake cottages and moving back to the town, once again I reluctantly put another of my iconic homes onto the market for less than the market price, anxious as I was to get back to London again.

When I returned to Bradford I found my cottage was decidedly the worse for wear, having been let for a year to a couple who had obviously given it little thought or attention. It would take me some time to sort it out again. Meanwhile, Nicky's friends and my sister, who was working for the NHS, were urging me to get Nicky sectioned and into hospital. It was something I was extremely loath to do, aware as I was of how adversely it might affect the career he had worked so hard for. He had by then got a degree in maths at Edinburgh University and gone on to gain a master's degree in econometrics at the London School of Economics. When I finally agreed there was no other course of action, as he was obviously in dire need of treatment, he was sectioned in the Hammersmith and Fulham mental hospital. When I gathered enough courage to go to see him in hospital in London, he appeared so obtuse and lost that it was impossible to communicate with him.

I'd had such high hopes for my son to go on and enjoy the fruits of his labours after he'd worked so hard and been so academic throughout his childhood. He should by now be reaping rewards, not being shut up without dignity in a dark snake-pit of a hospital. At this point I learned that a certain drug dealer had been supplying the boys with drugs when they were all students at St Paul's School in Hammersmith.

When Nicky left hospital he stayed with me for as long as it was thought wise, but it would take me many years of returning to therapy to come out of the depression I experienced in the wake of my son's illness. However, it did eventually turn out to have a beneficial outcome for me as it was due to Nicky that I was lucky enough to find, through the charity Mind, a counsellor called Bridget, who was to turn my life around as well as be there for me from then on to keep me on track. She was someone I could always rely on to put a different perspective on things when I became too caught up in destructive narratives. She was far more proficient at the job than any of the over-qualified analysts I'd seen in the past. I've heard counselling described as just 'sympathetic listening' but I feel that its success is down to the right kind of 'empathetic' listening, as well as the right kind of invaluable relationship that's created over time between two people: the patient and therapist.

Despite this, it wasn't until the ripe old age of sixty-six, when I joined Hibernia College in the autumn of 2006 to study art therapy, that I learnt more about mental health deviations, especially bipolar disorder. I had little time for the way they expected us to express the Rudolph Steiner method of painting though – the very thinnest amount of watercolour was required to be applied layer upon layer to a sheet of cartridge paper, tediously allowing each layer to dry in between each laborious process. To me, it proved too rigid a way in which to create. It was certainly not a satisfying way to paint for anyone with bipolar disorder. My way of painting has always been spontaneous and based on the premise that you wait for the muse to come to you, not force it slowly and excruciatingly to come to the fore.

Although I enjoyed the varied lectures, as well as my months of work practice at a clinic in Bristol at the end of the year, where I was allowed to treat two patients with their problems through their art, I was taken to task over some small unintentional errors, thereby barring me from progressing to another stage at the college. At this point I decided it wasn't for me. This might have been for the best, as it's quite probable I would have become much too engaged with my patients, which would have all too soon proved to their detriment, as well as mine. Nonetheless, I was disappointed that it didn't work out. But after all the lectures at the college on the subject of bipolar, I was at last slowly coming around to the idea that perhaps, after all, I was suffering with the disorder myself.

Some years ago at my medical surgery, I was prescribed a course of lithium and advised to contact a local therapist, who I soon realised knew even less than I did about the psyche, usually arriving in an agitated state to our sessions in her house, presumably trying to remember our last session and absently asking, 'And have you had any interesting dreams lately, Judy?'

During our sessions she would spend the first five minutes flicking furiously through her notebook, presumably trying to find her jottings of our previous session. But she did suggest that, as I'd had so little in the way of trust in my mother, I also counter-intuitively did the opposite of whatever advice she gave me, seeing her as my mother's transitional figure. In the end she suggested she pass me on to my next analyst – a male 'father' figure as she put it.

Bipolar disorder is notoriously difficult to diagnose, largely because it is so difficult to recognise in yourself. Any mention that you are behaving in a manic fashion, or suggestions that this may be an imbalance, are immediately dismissed in your current euphoric state, and such comments are often met with a barrage of expletives and aggressive irritation. This means you are rarely able to accept a prognosis of your condition and therefore any treatment to help you cope with it. With this particular disorder, you are frequently, and often critically, in denial – to your own detriment, especially as far as treatment is concerned.

And yet, by 2010, at the age of seventy, I finally fully accepted that I was a bipolar victim. In many ways it was an enormously freeing realisation. By then I had accepted it intellectually but it wasn't until I felt it emotionally that it finally sank into my psyche. For some while, the thoughts in my head swirled around as though they were many entangled clothes in the whirl of a washing machine, and as the cobwebs in my brain slowly shredded, it allowed me to see through the miasma and make some sense of my life and the many vicissitudes that had so often engulfed me. Now that many past incidents could be clarified, it allowed me to start coming to terms with the disorder and not let it tenaciously grab me by the throat and control me any longer; at last I could look forward to being more in charge of my life.

Not only that, but I was beginning to realise how often I'd attempted to solve a difficult atavistic relationship by setting up a similar juxtaposition within a current relationship. It would be in an unconscious, yet vain attempt to resolve what had hitherto been a disfunctional but critical relationship, making the current one similarly doomed to failure. Too much had been riding on the opposite sex and on relationships that should have been ancillary and not pivotal to my life. Now I finally began to discover that I could be self-reliant – I didn't need to continually seek affirmation. I could have a life where I could find my own solutions to ensure fulfilment.

Treatment

For many, treating bipolar presents an enormous challenge. The only thing people can do when in dire distress with a mental condition is consult a doctor, who may or may not prescribe medication and may suggest analytical therapy, for which there is an unendurably long waiting list and which is only of any benefit to someone who can afford the exorbitant fees an analyst can charge. It also remains to this day a profession that is not under statutory regulation and is only overseen and supported by various organisations, none of which are officially recognised by the government.

Although having stated in 2007 that the government intended to introduce statutory regulation for psychotherapists and counsellors, the Health & Care Professions Council (HCPC), which is independent of any professional body, later admitted at their meeting on 31 March 2011 that they had received a letter from Anne Milton MP (former parliamentary under-secretary of state) telling them that '…it is not currently our intention to proceed with statutory regulation of psychotherapists and counsellors'. A recent article online reported that the answer to the BBC investigation 'Can anyone call themselves a therapist or a counsellor' is yes. Currently the Government's preference, as set out in Enabling Excellence; an autonomy and accountability for Healthcare workers and social careers, is for voluntary registration, which means statutory regulation will only be considered where there is a 'compelling case' on the basis of public safety.

Indeed, even after paying for expensive therapy, which can take many years of weekly sessions, you are not even considered to have sufficiently reached the initial stage of 'transference' for at least the first two years. In psychoanalysis, transference is the term used for the displacement and redirection of emotions and attitudes from their original instinctual object onto a substitute, especially the therapist. Once the patient is thus in a dependent relationship with his analyst, the task of the therapist is to locate the underlying material and ensure it becomes unearthed for an interpretation of the hitherto repressed unconscious, which, it is said, reveals the patient's defences against anxiety. The work of the analyst is to break a patient down layer by layer to their most basic roots in order to bring to the surface these underlying disorders. It is psychologically akin to digging away at the flesh around a wound in order to find a bullet. Unfortunately, it leaves the patient walking around in a raw state until they can, over another period of time, be put back together again, hopefully in a more adaptive fashion.

Another possibility is finding a charity like Mind, which immeasurably helped me because I was eventually lucky enough to find someone who was empathetic, like Bridget. But while it is certainly more affordable, you are only likely to be allotted a limited number of sessions with a counsellor.

Other than that, continuous treatments are few and far between, and all this when you could be beside yourself and literally on the verge of suicide. Is it any wonder that bipolar has the highest death rate for any mental health disorder?

In the past, bipolar was treated quite drastically, often with lobotomy. This is a surgical intervention in which the nerve pathways in a lobe of the brain are severed from those in other areas, a radical therapeutic measure intended to calm patients with mental illness like schizophrenia and bipolar disorder. From the 1940s, lobotomy was seen as a miracle cure in the UK, despite opposition from some doctors, and especially psychoanalysts. It then became a mainstream treatment of psychiatry with more than 1,000 operations a year being performed at the peak of its popularity – mainly because the alternative was probably thought to be worse. Few patients were followed up afterwards to see how they were affected by the operation. The procedure was described by one psychiatrist as 'putting in a brain needle and stirring the works'. These gruesome instruments of torture consisted of an 8cm steel spike attached to a wooden handle and once represented the leading edge of psychiatric science, being seen as a miracle cure for a range of mental illnesses.

The most prolific lobotomist in the country, even the world, was a neurosurgeon called Sir Wylie McKissock based at the Atkinson Morley Hospital in Wimbledon. He was said to have performed at least 3,000 lobotomies, thinking of it as a 'five-minute procedure'. In 1949, Egas Moniz won the Nobel Prize for his invention of the lobotomy technique.

At that time patients would often find themselves in straitjackets and held in padded cells, as well as being subjected to physical violence. When I was working for a while in an NHS hospital for the occupational therapy department, I would sometimes have to visit the mental wards, where there was a spiral staircase winding down to a dark pit-like room below. I was told that at one time mental patients would be chained in the pit so that the public could come and gape at their antics for their weekend entertainment.

There followed a trend for electric shock treatment or electroconvulsive treatment (ECT), which means passing a strong electric current through the brain. It dates back to the 1930s and started out as an experiment after psychiatrists noticed some heavily distressed patients suddenly appeared to improve after an epileptic fit. It became a popular form of treatment in the 1960s and is still in use today, with around 4,000 patients still undergoing ECT if other medications appear to fail.

The patient is given general anaesthetic and a muscle relaxant, after which electrodes are placed on each side of the patient's head and the brain is given a series of electrical pulses, which are said to induce a seizure within the brain lasting approximately one minute. It has since been thought of as another tool of terror, since its image was tarnished in Ken Kesey's novel *One Flew Over the Cuckoo's Nest*. However, once again, experts are still uncertain as to how this treatment works. Many different theories have been suggested, but research hasn't shown exactly what effects it has or even how these extreme procedures might help with mental health problems. Despite this, it continues to be used as a form of treatment as it is believed to act by temporarily altering some of the brain's electromagnetic processes: a distinctly alarming reflection on many of the old haphazard, hit-or-miss measures that are still in use today.

No one really knew what these appalling procedures really did to a patient afterwards, as few of them were followed up, but many ended up forever mentally and emotionally dulled.

Medication

But what of today? Currently, bipolar disorder is usually treated with medication and therapy or counselling. The usual medication treatments are a number of drugs or 'mood stabilisers', in particular selective serotonin reuptake inhibitors (SSRIs). Serotonin is a neurotransmitter (a messenger chemical that carries signals between nerve cells in the brain), which is reported to have a good influence on mood, emotion and sleep – hence the popularity of Prozac (or fluoxetine), which was popularly prescribed as an anxiety disorder drug in the USA to treat depression in a blanket procedure in the 1980s. The latest SSRI is Cipralex (escitalopram), which so far is said to be the best performing.

Recent findings, while stating that psychiatry has long sought and failed to find a compelling medical explanation for depression, note that the emphasis on serotonin can be said to have some scientific foundation, even if the latest evidence appears to suggest that SSRIs like escitalopram are only marginally better than a placebo and are often met with non-compliance from patients. They also appear to have unpleasant side effects and produce feelings of sluggishness.

The major clinical problem with medication for bipolar patients is that prescribing pills is unlikely to work for both the manic and the depressive states – even should the patient be prepared to engage with the idea of medication. When a patient is in the depressive stage and desperate to find a way out of the oppressive darkness that is so overwhelming, any kind of chemical intervention is welcome. However, as soon as you re-emerge into the light again, any medication that is a reminder of your depressive state will be dispensed with. When you are euphorically soaring into the stratosphere again, you will immediately dispose of anything that might hamper your exhilarating flight. And this is only if you have progressed enough to admit you are suffering from a disability and given in to the idea of being medicated in the first place.

Speaking for myself, this stage of bipolar is a highly seductive one. It is as if you are walking on air while experiencing an arousing surge of serotonin, dopamine and noradrenaline. However, even when high on self-induced chemicals, there is a fear that taking medication while high might result in missing the creative spark that is the holy grail of your creative aspirations.

For me, the major problem with medication for my bipolar has always been that diagnosing it as an illness and prescribing pills is only likely to work when I'm in a dysfunctional state and desperate to find a way out of the engulfing darkness that is the hallmark of depression. As soon as the medication starts to take effect and I re-emerge from the darkness, I immediately dispense with any medication prescribed to me and, throwing caution to the wind, once more strike out 'where angels fear to tread'. The last thing I want when I feel myself soaring back into the dazzling light again is something that I associate with depression.

Author and Psychiatrist Douglas Bey Jr who wrote *Loving a Depressed Man* points out that people only seek out help when they are depressed but when they are on a high they resent their huge energy being slowed down by medication. When you are treating creative people you have to carefully moderate their medication otherwise they will feel their creativity is being stifled. He further explains that many people who have the disorder, will attempt to self-medicate which only aggravates and compounds the problem

Personally, I have always resisted being on drugs for any length of time, being determined not to fall into the trap of becoming substance dependent. And, having experienced a bad trip after being offered a 'home-grown' drug that resulted in a doctor's visit to bring me down, I have also steered clear of the drug scene. Since I had decided to base my faith in therapy, how would I know if I was making any progress if I was constantly medicated?

It isn't as though much progress has been made with current medications over the years, as it is not thought to be financially cost-effective enough for big pharma, the pharmaceutical giants, to invest in such programmes. For them, it's not considered worth the trouble to stage sufficient research projects on the subject.

Lithium

When I was in a particular depressive state and contacted a doctor, I would usually be prescribed lithium. Lithium is a chemical element and appears as number 3 on the periodic table, symbolised by the letters Li and located among the alkali metals. It is a compound that late in the twentieth century was an important component of battery electrolytes and electrodes – certain types of lithium are used as high-energy additives to rocket propellants. Lithium metal is corrosive and requires special handling to avoid skin contact. It is primarily used to treat bipolar disorder and major depressive disorders that don't improve when following the usage of antidepressants. It's contended that 'it reduces the risk of suicide'. Taken in tablet form orally, it is said to act on a person's nervous system (brain and spinal cord). Doctors admit they don't know exactly how lithium works to stabilise a person's mood, but it is thought to help strengthen nerve cell connections in brain regions that are involved in regulating mood, thinking and behaviour.

It is, however, difficult to imagine how it was decided that it might have properties that could prove of use to certain bipolar patients. Their brew of choice is more likely to be alcohol or illegal opiates when it comes to self-medicating – surely no more harmful than a battery component chemical.

The side effects of lithium are hand tremors, increased thirst, weight gain, vomiting and diarrhoea, as well as impairment of memory and poor concentration. Its effect on me was to make my mouth feel dry and my mind hazy. The other side effect is that it dangerously harms your kidneys if taken regularly over a long period.

A certain Dr Lewis Judd and his colleagues concluded that:

> Lithium often induces subjective feelings of
> cognitive slowing, together with decreased
> ability to learn, concentrate and memorize…
> including decrements on various cognitive
> tests, which includes memory tests.

In a more recent study on the subject he found 'substantial detrimental effects of lithium on associational processing in patients with manic-depressive illness.'

More up-to-date medications have shown to be effective in various ways. Mood stabilisers work by decreasing the amount of abnormal activity in the brain. Anticonvulsant or anti-seizure medications, apparently first developed to treat disorders like epilepsy, are also sometimes used as mood stabilisers. But it's very much a personal quest to find what works for you as an individual, as each person's needs are different and people react differently to medication – there is no 'one size fits all'. This is especially true as the disorder itself poses a very difficult conundrum, not only necessitating the need to balance the extremity of the manias, but conversely to also counterbalance the despair of the depression – all this while not turning the patient into a moron.

Hospitalisation

In serious cases where there is a risk to self or others, involuntary hospitalisation is felt to be necessary. However, hospital stays are now shorter than they were in previous times, while outsourced crisis teams will visit a patient at home as well as take on the job of the administration of drugs and possible further care.

Crisis teams can help those with mental health issues when there might otherwise be a need for hospitalisation – for instance, in the case of a psychosis or severe self-harm or suicide issues. The team can include a number of mental health professions, such as a psychiatrist, mental health nurses, social workers and support workers. However, crisis teams did not exist in my day, and although I sought other types of treatments for myself, like analysis, I was only to be hospitalised twice briefly during mid-life breakdowns.

My son, Nicky, however, was hospitalised on many occasions. On one of these I had to give my consent just before my plane left for a holiday to Egypt. I was stuck in the corridor waiting for the call from the doctor just as my plane was boarding. It was vital to me that he get long-term treatment.

Fortunately, I managed to make it to the plane just in time, but I was fairly worn down by then with all the drama and worry. Although it was a fascinating journey through ancient history and I was blown away with the beauty of tomb paintings and antiquities, I was glad to get home again and get the latest news of Nicky. So the first thing I did when I reached Heathrow airport was to phone Leon for news.

When Nicky was about to be released from hospital I booked a hotel near the one where he had been placed in London. It was the first time I'd set eyes on him in seven years and he was much changed. He looked worn down and lost and it was a shock to realise how much of his confidence had been eroded. He was in a state of deep depression and I did what I could to lift his mood and get him settled into a house share.

How could this happen to my beautiful son who seemed to have everything going for him and whose life had showed such promise? If it was brutal for me to witness it, what must it have been like for him? In some ways he appeared numb – a state I could remember and fully empathise with.

The next Easter was spent with Nicky, Leon and his girlfriend in Brighton and afterwards I brought Nicky back to stay with me for a while, but he was still in the grip of a depression and desperately low. It would appear he could no longer manage to hold a job down, despite his high qualifications. Since I'd last seen him, he hadn't been able to stay put anywhere for long. Displaying typical behaviour for bipolar, he was unable to settle and when he decided to sell the flat he had painstakingly bought for himself in London when he was working, he bought a car and travelled the length and breadth of Britain.

For me, it was a terrifying period of receiving calls at all hours – sometimes from the police, informing me they had arrested my son but refusing to give me any information as to why, and sometimes intermittent reports from Nicky himself to tell me how he had been beaten up by the police and was in custody. I would then not hear from him for weeks. His brother Leon was my support throughout, and I'd have undoubtedly been in pieces if I hadn't had his calm help to call upon during those many difficult years. Nicky was finally sectioned in a closed-ward London hospital for up to six months, but once again was released earlier than expected.

I searched the internet and found *A Textbook of Psychiatry*, and under the heading of 'Hospitalisation' it states:

> It is almost always best to admit a patient suffering from mania or hypomania, as a psychiatric inpatient. Despite the patient protesting a willingness to take medication in the community, the lack of insight that occurs in this disorder, together with the feeling of well-being that often accompanies it, is very likely to lead to non-compliance and a risk of the mania worsening. As mentioned above, severe mania can lead to a dangerous level of self-neglect and dehydration… Relatives of previous sufferers are usually very pleased for admissions to take place, having witnessed its social and medical effects.

It's true that it was a relief to know my son was safe in hospital and no longer likely to harm himself or anyone else – at least during the time the staff could keep him there. Nevertheless, when they did manage to make him stay, he would generally be released early, having been rapidly de-toxified and therefore in a nervous and chronic state of depression.

According to him, each time he was sectioned, it would start with the police picking him up forcibly, while he tried to defend himself and flee in fear, then throwing him into a cell after aggressively manhandling him. Recently it's become the law to hospitalise someone showing mental health symptoms immediately, although the police still appear to use brute force to get them there.

This brutal process serves to completely take away a person's human dignity and, in the process, de-humanises them. Being physically forced into an institution is like being jailed, and going 'cold turkey' overnight to address substance dependency is a deeply unpleasant way to detox. Patients are then forced to take another kind of medication, one maybe only different from what they have used to self-medicate in that it's a legal substance. They are not told how the medication works, because no one knows that. If a patient refuses to take the medication and has another breakdown, they are warned that they would then be judged 'non-compliant' and be henceforth put on a more severe, and therefore longer, sectioning. In this way, they become gradually and thoroughly worn down and 'hospitalised' the longer they are kept in confinement.

You might think that negotiating with a psychiatrist who has your future in his hands is a rare experience, but that is not so – this is happening to approximately 60,000 people in the UK each year, and the number is rising.

If you are admitted under section two of the Mental Health Act, you are expected to stay in hospital for twenty-eight days, after which they must either release you or put you under a section three, when they can hold you for up to six months, although this can be extended. The decision is all within the power of your psychiatrist, while, as a patient, any objections you might make are believed to lack insight because you are deemed incapable of making a well-judged decision.

When he was finally released, Nicky was still in self-denial, having inherently lost any faith in the health system – and indeed in any system – and feeling not only extremely angry but appalled at his treatment. As a result of all this, he would refuse to attend out-patient crisis teams for medication, and once more the old revisionist cycle would start over again.

Therapy

Kay Redfield asserts that bipolar disorder worsens over time, so she strongly recommends medication. If not medicated after a period of time the chemical balance of the brain will change due to recurrent manic and depressive episodes, she says. Also secondary problems will occur should self-medication with drugs or alchohol have taken place. This has not necessarily been my experience, having at last come to terms with the disorder through many years of talking therapy. I have been able to keep some sort of a handle on it as long as I pace myself on a daily basis. I don't therefore feel the need to rely on drugs, which always come with a range of side effects that I find disturbing. Presumably Redfield is alluding to those further down the spectrum than myself.

She also points out that 'creatives' often choose for themselves how they should be treated. Saying that it's clear that intense human emotions play a part in the creative outlet in the arts. She adds that modern medicine now allows choices not previously available by treating the extreme feelings that can go with it like despair, turmoil and psychosis.

Of course, writers, artists and composers in the past didn't have much of a choice.

Speaking for myself, I can only recommend talking therapy as an immeasurable help to not only come to terms with your situation, but to allow you an opportunity to uncover some of your most deep-seated problems that may well have triggered the disorder in the first place. It can also help to change your perception of past and present events that may have had a seriously negative effect on you, while giving you the chance to appreciate the possible adverse effects that other people have unconsciously projected onto you due to their own problems. It gives you the opportunity to discuss personal issues in the safe ambiance of a consulting room, these being the stresses that may aggravate your condition. It is also an opportunity to learn awareness of your own mood cycles and how to recognise them before they become too severe. But, of course, it takes time to seek out the right therapist, and especially one you can afford long term.

I was passed on to Simon, my second therapist, after my first female therapist didn't work out. He had originally qualified as a doctor and had then trained as an analyst in Zurich in the Carl Jung Institute. He was a typically eccentric type of upper-class gentleman who had gained prestigious awards during his time at Oxford University as well as training to go into the church. Although much of his advice was somewhat over-laced with analytical jargon, which I often found difficult to decipher, he was a kind, helpful and reliable presence in my life during some of my most difficult years and saw me through many a dark night of the soul. But it was high time for me to get to work on my own problems, and I obviously had plenty of scope.

Other treatments

Recently, the BBC announced during some of their news updates that psilocybin, a constituent of 'magic mushrooms', is a possible help for depression. For years it's been suggested that psychedelic drugs could be a natural way to treat mental disorders, while the powers that be, as well as moral objections and litigation issues, have prevented the idea from being developed. An early-stage study has now suggested that 'magic mushrooms' are at least as good at reducing symptoms of depression as conventional treatments. According to a report from Imperial College if the drug is taken in high doses it has the ability to alter conscious awareness with vivid and elaborate visions as well as releasing memories and suppressed feelings. It also has the potential to alter the neocortex, the most evolutionarily developed aspect of our brain.

If such a treatment, alongside professional psychological support, could take us away from outdated and myopic 'drug-alone' perspectives that have dominated psychiatry for decades and towards a multi-level 'biopsychosocial' model, it could be a large step forward for psychiatry.

Another psychedelic experience currently popular with some wishing for an altered state that can last for some hours is a drug known as ayahuasca – also known as the tea, the vine and la purga. It is a brew made from the leaves of the *Psychotria viridis* shrub along with the stalks of the *Banisteriopsis caapi* vine. Many have travelled to foreign destinations, mostly in the jungles of South America, to experience taking the psychoactive drug and, while some have found it enlightening, others have found it downright distressing. The tea is traditionally prepared for the participant by a shaman, who needs to be standing by, as this powerful psychedelic brew affects the central nervous system and can not only cause severe bouts of nausea in the early stages but can lead to an altered state of consciousness that can include hallucinations, out-of-body experiences and euphoria.

Despite international evidence now suggesting the medicinal effectiveness of psychedelic drugs to treat mental health conditions, *The Guardian* reported recently that the Australian Therapeutic Drug Association (TGA) has made an interim decision that MDMA (Ecstacy) and psilocybin (magic mushrooms) are not to be rescheduled to the list of controlled medicines. The reclassification would have allowed them to be used in clinical therapy for those suffering from depression and post-traumatic stress disorder, (PTSD) as well as other mental disorders that are resistant to current medication. However, clinical trials have been given a $15 million grant by the TGA to continue with the research into psychedelics. CBD will eventually go on sale in Australia but first manufacturers will have to prove it works. CBD stands for cannabidiol and is the second most prevalent of the active ingredients of cannabis or marijuana. It is not to be confused with Tetrahydrocannabinol (THC) another natural compound of the cannabis genus, which can cause the 'high' sensations.

In the same article in *The Guardian*, Dr Arthur Christopoulos, dean of Monash University's faculty of pharmacy and pharmaceutical sciences in Australia, is quoted as saying that the government had realised the 'Achilles' heel' to treating the mental health tsunami is the lack of new and truly effective medicines to treat mental illness. 'Every single psychiatric drug on the market is based on research that is at least 50 years old,' he states. Anxiety disorders are the most common mental illnesses, affecting more than 14% of (Australian) adults each year, along with depression and substance abuse disorders. Evidence suggests that up to 12% of Australians experience PTSD during their lifetime. A recent *Observer* article stated that it has been estimated that up to 1.4 million people in the UK use cannabis for medical purposes mostly for three rare childhood epilepsies. Experts predict it will eventually become available for many other types of epilepsy. The entire UK cannabis market could be worth billions if recreational use is also legalised.

The isolation problem

Of course, one of the problems with treating bipolar patients is that they often withdraw from society just at the point that they need intervention. If others make it clear that they see your behaviour as inappropriate and refuse to acknowledge your grandiose ideas, it can bring on an irrational rage. You become angry because you feel others are trying to put you down by purposely refusing to accept your unconventional ideas – your anger and fear are projected onto them, making them the object of your paranoia. Thus you are convinced that everyone is conspiring against you. It becomes a vicious circle and just another reason for you to hide away and become isolated from the very society you so badly need in order to find some sort of solace. At this stage, you would not wish this disorder on your worst enemy; you are in a dark valley.

In prehistoric tribes, depression itself could have served a tribe by causing an unhealthy individual to move himself onto the outer edges of the group, thereby not adversely threatening the group's health and survival rate. In this way it is possible that depression could have had an evolutionary advantage for our forebears when it encouraged them to isolate at a time when they needed to allow their bodies to deal with any bacterial inflammation. But unfortunately what might have benefited humans long ago is now affecting our current society with the risk of ensuing bouts of melancholy. We should not be relying on heuristic shortcuts and outdated circuits that were originally adapted for the savannah.

It's also possible that those with mental health problems even today feel the urge to isolate themselves from evolutionary competition, which still seems to be prejudiced in favour of maximising survivability, when it's a question of the need to co-operate with one another. In considering teamwork projects or even future relationships, we have developed deep-seated instincts that immediately assist us in deciding who to trust as far as our health is concerned.

We quickly and unconsciously size up a new acquaintance as to whether we can get along with them or whether they are going to fit in with our lifestyle as well as with our social group. To ignore this might put us in a position where we are forced away from our usual community should we violate their mores. We could then find ourselves as outsiders too and find we can no longer rely on our community for support in a crisis.

Many people with mental disorders are not like other people. Their disposition is often anarchistic and rebellious, making others feel uneasy in their company as well as making them objects of ridicule. Their behaviour feels unfamiliar and even threatening to others. However, at such times they vitally need to find a coping skill that does not end up isolating them. But if they are unwell it's difficult for them to be sufficiently sociable to fit in and so they end up cloistering themselves for their own protection, fearing that they will be shunned or incarcerated forever. They stay in their rooms, or they go and live somewhere isolated or find professions where their inconsistencies won't stand out, which usually means searching for a solitary working environment. At all cost they want to avoid being hospitalised or imprisoned, thereby losing what fragments they have been able to retain of their human dignity and self-respect.

Another reason for isolation is the shame they feel, with their acute awareness that they are unacceptable because of their idiosyncratic behaviour. Shame is what drives them to keep themselves to themselves in the dark corners of society, staying as unnoticed as possible. They know they need to co-operate to survive, necessitating being even a small part of the group, so this is a way of compromising and protecting themselves. These are the people who spend most of their time watching TV or films or interacting online in fantasy situations with others who cannot harm them from a distance. They hope to be able to work out eventually how to fit into society and not be at risk of having their self-esteem eroded further. But in the meantime they try to stay safe by distancing themselves from society so that society won't completely throw them out, and ultimately destroy them.

So what is the solution for people suffering from a mental illness that either plunges them into a depressive state so that they feel the need to isolate, and which society treats very harshly, or raises them into a creative 'high' that means they reject treatment? And should we be seeking to cure bipolar anyway? There is strong evidence to suggest that many sufferers don't want to be 'cured' – they desire simply to be better understood. Is sectioning and hospitalisation, often by coercive means, really the way we want to go on treating people who are observably unwell in the twenty-first century? Perhaps, after all, there is a better way to show compassion to others who are forced to constantly struggle with a difficult and sometimes dangerous disability.

Chapter 6

CURE OR MANAGE?

Nicky would continue to be sectioned in different hospitals over the course of the next fifteen years. At the beginning, I would plead with his doctors, and nurses – anyone I could find, to help him. Nevertheless, he consistently walked out of hospitals where he'd been sectioned. When they did eventually put him on a locked ward, he would invariably be released too quickly and in a chronic state of depression, having received little in the way of any talking treatment to help alleviate any of his underlying problems. He would then be persuaded to attend a crisis team's community programme near to where he lived at that time for medication, which he would take while depressed and, like many a bipolar sufferer before him, dispense with as soon as his mood lightened, only for the same pattern to be repeatedly played out, over and over again.

Bipolar is one of the most difficult and problematic disorders to live with, and during its depressive periods it can prove chronic. It's difficult also for those who have to care for the victim, and especially heart-breaking for a family member to watch their loved one suffer with the illness and be frustratingly unable to help them. This is especially hard when they refuse to admit to it and think they can deal with it alone, usually leading them to search for some sort of illegal substance to self-medicate and numb the pain, only compounding the problem.

Friends usually move away as they are not able to stand by once again and have their advice and offers of help ignored and often thrown back at them. Parents, and particularly mothers, are the ones who come in for the most abuse, as it is felt they are ones who are most likely to take it. Sometimes, it is necessary to keep yourself at arm's length, if only to preserve your own sanity should all advice fall on deaf ears or be received with insulting behaviour.

Nevertheless, society needs to find ways to treat bipolar sufferers with the compassion they require in order for them to deal with their mood swings, by providing funds to research better medication and by making vital and all-important talking therapies more available and affordable. Should they be allowed some of these crucial life-giving requirements, what more could these gifted and creative folk, who are day by day dealing with the disturbing effects of bipolar disorder, achieve for us as a society?

A recent article in *The Observer* entitled 'Doctors fear new child mental health crisis' sets out that paediatricians, psychologists and charitable groups providing mental health support predicted that there would be a huge surge in cases of mental illness when the lockdown for Covid was finally lifted, although for some reason, it was not immediately apparent that this was the case. One suggestion for this was that being at home around family or other familiar people was less stressful than coping with life outside the home.

However, that said, some charitable mental health services said they had seen a 70% rise in demand in 2020 compared with the previous year. The number experiencing eating disorders, self harm and even psychosis is causing serious concern. It goes on to suggest that one in six children now have mental health issues and says that in England in November 2020 referrals to children's and young people's health services were at a record high, representing a 66%

increase on the same month in 2019 and 139% increase on the same period in 2017.

Although a large sum of money from the Department of Health is apparently going to be provided to help, I would imagine many of the cases referred to in *The Observer* article are likely to be bipolar disorder cases in the making. If we don't as a society learn more about this capricious disorder that can set you apart and destabilise your life, when so much could be gained from them for society by mobilising and encouraging the positive side of it, what does it say about us? Do we really want to see our children growing up feeling lost, sad, confused, anxious and disorientated, as pointed out in the newspaper article?

The toll on the UK's mental health caused by the pandemic will obviously become clearer in the future in the years after the lockdown has been lifted. But to return to the Royal College of Psychiatrists' warning, which strongly applies to children, there were 80,226 more under-18s referred to NHS mental health services in England between April and December 2020 than in the same period in 2019. The number of children and young people needing emergency care rose 20% to 18,269 while the number of adults needing emergency treatment reached a record high of 159,347. However, it was later reported that there were fewer suicide calls during the long lockdown during the Covid pandemic, which was put down to the idea that in a crisis of that sort, people usually pull together.

According to an article in *The Guardian*:

> Parity of esteem for mental health was
> supposedly enshrined in law in the 2012
> Health and Social Care Act. But the promise
> was not fulfilled. Five years later, Theresa
> May named the lack of support for people
> with mental illnesses as one of the 'burning

injustices' that she hoped her premiership
would address. But the prospect of measures
such as legal limits on waiting times for
talking therapies, which have long been in
place for A&E and other hospital treatments,
appears more remote than ever.

Apparently more than a third of children and adolescents referred for treatment received none, while another third waited more than a year. Additional emotional problems relating to bereavement, loss and loneliness will obviously only add to these issues in the coming years. However, it has been reported that Catherine, the Duchess of Cambridge has launched her own Centre for Early Childhood to raise awareness of the importance of children's early years and help transform lives from the important formative years onwards. She says she wants to create a happier, more mentally healthy, more nurturing society.

Is bipolar a defect?

The first question to raise is whether, despite its at times debilitating symptoms, bipolar can indeed be seen as a defect. Included in a study of the evolutionary advantages of bipolar disorder is an article entitled 'Positive Traits in the Bipolar Spectrum regarding Bipolar Spectrum and Evolution' by Tiffany A. Greenwood, an associate professor at the University of California, San Diego. Her study stipulates that bipolar must have a purpose in society since it has persisted for so long and while having a high heritability and widespread prevalence which might make it questionable with regards to evolution theory, it has not been pruned by natural selection from the gene pool.

Other evolutionary models relating to balancing selection and fitness trade-offs have been widely debated. For example, it has been suggested that traits associated with bipolar disorder and psychosis may provide fitness advantages in terms of sexual selection, mating success or social skills, especially within certain groups.

If some of the more beneficial traits of bipolar disorder could be understood by the public, it could help to erase the stigma of a severe mental disability such as bipolar. Greenwood lists positive psychological traits such as spirituality, empathy, realism, creativity and resilience which are frequently observed in such individuals.

She suggests that if the more positive aspects of the disorder are better recognised, and ways of enhancing these traits are explored, there is some chance of clinical improvement for those with the problem. Who knows where their creative skills might take them if there was found a way to help them to subdue some of the more disturbing and distracting elements of their disorder?

On the subject of future treatment, Greenwood seems to back this up by making the point that current treatments concentrate more on controlling the disorder rather than facilitating the patient's creative needs and artistic potential. Creative expression is a positive and healthy way for people to express themselves, especially those struggling with a stumbling block like bipolar.

She also makes the point that bipolar patients often discontinue their medications due to their fear of 'diminished creativity', among some of the other unpleasant side effects of the drug. Some patients, including myself, once stabilised on lithium, will even decrease their own dosage in the name of creative expression, or dispense with the drug in the nearest bin.

It appears that many others with the disorder find it not only enjoyable in certain phases but so integral to their creative work that they prefer to go untreated rather than risk limiting or losing it, although I would rather know that I will be able to sleep at night, something that sometimes feels like a battle ground. In a recent article by David Engleman, the neuroscientist and author, he suggests that each area of the brain is in competition with the other and since we lose our sight at night our visual system compensates by providing dreams to keep it from being taken over. Dreams are the brain's way of defending that territory. It could explain a lot for me.

The Greenwood article continues to point out the negative aspects of those with the disorder refusing treatment, and suggests that a study between creativity and bipolar would produce a better understanding of the needs of a sufferer and promote more sympathetic treatment thereby leading to more compliance from the patient.

To me, this last point is one of the most important of Greenwood's article, as she points out that we must treat those with the disorder with more care and try to appreciate their needs. They are obviously incapable of fitting in with the conventional norm as it has been organised for a certain middle strata, but this certainly does not diminish their importance to society. It's also true to say the world expects everyone to be a functioning and contributing member of society, but for many this is not always possible. Sometimes it can be hard to tolerate a person who has a mental disorder – they don't react like other people and it's difficult to know what's going on in their heads, and intuitively we rarely fail to recognise that they are different and should not be unfairly labelled as disabled.

Gene editing

But could there come a time when society makes the decision to erase this disruptive disorder and eliminate its effect on us forever? Looking forward to a time when we are able to detect where the bipolar disorder gene resides on the DNA double helix spiral system, that all life is composed of and then editing it while still in its embryonic form, it certainly seems possible. Of course, we still haven't discovered where the mind is in our brain, nor indeed the mythical soul. But mankind is ever ingenious and nothing will stop progress and our inherent desire to control whatever it is we discover.

A new method of gene editing called CRISPR (clustered regularly interspaced short palindromic repeats) has been developed by Jennifer Doudna and Emmanuelle Charpentier, winning them the Nobel Prize in chemistry in 2020. It was a significant breakthrough in biotechnology and medicine as it allows for the genomes to be edited 'in vivo' (in living creatures) with extremely high precision, and with ease.

Of course, I can't mention this without pointing out that it was not only a historic event for science but also for feminists, as it marked the first time two women had won the award without any male contribution.

Moving on, the race it seems is now on to work prenatally, interfering directly with the embryo pre-birth. A handful of teams have apparently begun to explore this process, aiming to make precise edits to genes, but such studies are still rare and generally strictly regulated. Fortunately, in all studies where researchers used embryos for scientific purposes only, they did not generate as pregnancies. Nonetheless, there are obviously certain safety concerns, as it's possible such interferences could create a permanent change that could then be passed down through many generations to follow. But there's usually someone in the world who is brazenly prepared to take the risk of developing scientific discoveries prematurely.

However, should that awesome time come about – or should I say when? – wouldn't that then rob society of some of its most intensely and intrinsically colourful characters, the people who can reach beyond the usual perimeters of rationality and reason, going 'where angels fear to tread' and then ingeniously providing us with their invaluable insights brought about by their original and creative ways of perceiving them? Notwithstanding, do we even have a handle on what reality really is? As far as we know, it seems to be something on which everyone appears to have distinctly diverse perspectives.

Eugenics and the artistic temperament

So, now that we are entering an age where we can alter and edit our genes with comparative ease, and in time, no doubt, even while a baby is still in its embryonic state, how soon will we be likely to detect the gene that represents bipolar or the manic-depressive illness? And when we do, how will the arguments flow considering our horror and distaste for eugenics?

'Eugenics' as such, literally means 'good creation'. The ancient Greek philosopher Plato may have been the first person to promote the idea, although the term 'eugenics' didn't come on the scene until British scholar Sir Francis Galton coined it in 1883 in his book *Inquiries into Human Faculty and its Development*. Should we blame Plato then, when in one of his best-known literary works, *The Republic,* he wrote about creating a superior society by encouraging the procreation of high-class people while discouraging coupling between the lower classes. He also suggested a variety of mating rules to help create an optimal society. But then didn't Nietzsche promote the idea that we should all live life to the full. 'Dare to become what we are. Of course the weak will go under but isn't that to be welcomed,' he postulated. His fellow philosopher Karl Marx was also in agreement.

That's not to forget more recent happenings in Sweden, when more than 60,000 Swedish women, branded as low class and mentally slow, were rounded up and were sterilised from 1935 until as late as 1976 apparently by a string of Social Democratic government politicians.

However, these acts cannot be confined to Scandinavia alone, according to Jonathan Freedland in *The Guardian* in August 1997, who pointed out:

> Eugenics is a dirty little secret of the
> (political) left. The names of the first
> champions read like a roll call of British
> socialism's best and brightest: Sidney and
> Beatrice Webb, George Bernard Shaw,
> Harold Laski, John Maynard Keynes, Marie
> Stopes, the *New Statesman* and even
> lamentably the *Manchester Guardian*.

Freedland goes on to say that British polymath Bertram Russell had also suggested in his time that the state (should) issue colour-coded procreation tickets. Apparently those with the wrong colour ticket would then be fined, if caught in the act.

The aim of eugenics is said to be to reduce human suffering by 'breeding out' disease, disabilities and so-called undesirable characteristics from the human population. Modern eugenics, however, is now more often referred to as human genetic engineering, and CRISPR in particular as 'molecular scissors', and has certainly come a long way – scientifically and ethically – offering hope for treating many devastating genetic illnesses like Huntington's or sickle cell disease.

'Gene therapy' has been a goal ever since scientists first began learning how to edit genes in the 1970s. But it's never been possible on any scale until now because editing one gene among approximately 21,000 others in the DNA of each of our cells is nigh on impossible. It needs accurate tools for finding the right gene then snipping it at that precise point and stitching in a new gene in its place. While biologists have been able to make such edits for some time, they were not able to make them with any degree of accuracy for clinical use until now. If editing is too messy or inadvertently alters other genes too, the consequences could be dire, as an unintended edit could even trigger cancer.

Even so, such methods obviously remain highly controversial. Historically, eugenics by any other name encouraged people of so-called healthy superior stock to reproduce and discouraged reproduction of the mentally challenged or anyone who fell outside the social norm. Eugenics was popular in America during much of the first half of the twentieth century, yet it earned its more recent negative association mainly from Adolf Hitler's obsessive attempts to create a superior Aryan race, creating a devastating world war and the loss of more than a generation of young men.

CRISPR has changed all that. The technique uses an enzyme molecule called Cas9, first found in bacteria, which can be reliably programmed to find its target. It carries with it a piece of genetic material called mRNA, similar to DNA, which holds the secret of the target site. When the enzyme finds the DNA sequence matching that on its mRNA reference strand, it snips the DNA double helix in two. Other enzymes can then insert another piece of DNA, encoding the 'healthy' sequence into the break.

CRISPR also made gene editing more viable for medicine. In a recent *Observer* article, Jennifer Doudna stated:

> The first diseases researchers are looking for
> are those that require a simple change in a

single gene and in a cell or tissue that we
can target easily. As it's a new and expensive
approach, it makes sense to prioritise
diseases for which no other treatments exist.

A team from MIT and Harvard University in the USA conducted CRISPR experiments on mice that had been genetically altered to carry the human form of progeria, which causes very rapid ageing and eventual death in children born with a mutation gene called lamin A. This is a disease that alters all the cells in a body, but after the mice were treated when fourteen days old, they were found to live into old age, causing great excitement. The head of the team commented:

> Five years ago the prospect of correcting a
> single base pair in a living animal that
> causes a fatal genetic disease with a one-
> time treatment of an engineered molecular
> machine seemed like science fiction.

Apparently, CRISPR therapy may first see wide clinical use for erasing neurological genetic conditions such as Huntingdon's disease, because brain tissue turns out to be easier to edit than muscle. Although widespread clinical use of CRISPR therapies is still five to ten years down the line, Doudna admits to being 'constantly amazed at how quickly genome research is being adopted around the world'.

While bipolar disorder has obviously wreaked havoc on my family, I would still plead for caution when it comes to CRISPR being let loose on our DNA, certainly with regard to bipolar disorder. Oswald Bumke (1877–1950) belonged to a generation of psychiatrists who took the union of psychiatry and neurology for granted and was specifically interested in manic depressive disorders. He rejected psychoanalysis as 'being imprisoned within the confines of materialism' and considered psychotherapy 'an art that depended on the nature of its practitioner rather than on technique'. Bumke's *Handbuch der Geisteskrankheiten* (Handbook of Mental Diseases) and other works on the fundamental problems of medicine have retained their value to the present day. On 1 April 1924 he became the chair of the psychiatry department at the University of Munich and the director of the university clinic. These appointments arguably made him the most prominent psychiatrist in Germany, marking a striking generational change of direction in Munich, and in German psychiatry as a whole, at the time.

Even though it is reported that at one time he supported sterilisation during the Nazi era as well as advocating it in his book *The State and Mental Diseases,* nonetheless Bumke appeared to turn away from it when he had this to say:

If we could extinguish the sufferers from
manic depressive psychosis from the world,
we would at the same time deprive ourselves
of an immeasurable amount of the
accomplished and good, of colour and
warmth of spirit and freshness.

Dr John W. Robertson, while writing on Edgar Allan Poe, surmised that the mind and its reactions were too complex to ever be fully understood or controlled. Furthermore, he felt that for the world as a whole this was a good thing, 'however high an inheritance tax the victims of heredity must pay.' He suggested that should we stamp out everything that leads to nervousness. close mating of neurotics, or even insanity and various forms of degeneracy, we would have a race of stoics - leading to men incapable of imagination, ingeniousness or souls with personality. 'Who could or would breed for a hump-backed Pope or a clubfooted Byron, a scrofulous Keats or

a soul obsessed Poe. Nature has done fairly well by us' he
feels.

Managing bipolar

In my view, bipolar doesn't need to be cured so much as
managed. Commenting on the latest finding by Professor
Smith in *The Guardian*, Suzanne Hudson, chief executive
of Bipolar UK, the online bipolar support group, said:

> Given the rise in requests for support from
> parents and families of children to 'Bipolar
> UK', research that helps identify young
> people more at risk of developing bipolar
> disorder is vitally important.

The Guardian article also says,

> I suspect there are things that can be done
> early on to help someone at high risk of
> bipolar, such as making certain lifestyle
> changes, protecting sleep patterns and
> avoiding certain stresses. The sooner we can
> intervene in bipolar the better the outcome.

These kinds of findings could be of exceptional interest to
bipolar sufferers, who have for so long been shouldering
the burden of their often volatile disorder. Perhaps bipolar,
as well as other mental disorders, could even be considered
to be our brain's preparation for its next evolutionary leap,
an event that is hardly likely to metamorphose without
considerable upheaval.

Could the brain's inevitable desire to mutate to the next
level since it expanded from the reptilian and Neanderthal
brain mean we are on the cusp of our next evolutionary
leap? The human brain is the largest brain in proportion to
our body size of any living creature, and also the most

complex. It uses at least 20% of the body's energy. Although the brain's ability to grow in size is obviously restricted by the size of the birth canal, could it be that in its consistent desire to evolve, despite its limited space, the brain frequently overcharges and subsequently blows a fuse, resulting in what we currently term as mental disorder?

There are specific genes that control the size of the human brain, and these genes continue to play a role in brain evolution, implying that the brain is continuing to evolve, although this is still a contentious subject. Human brain evolution can also happen by different methods, like natural selection and genetic drift.

On the subject of natural selection and evolution; Dr Benjamin Hunt from the University of Birmingham explains that while technology and culture may alter the strength and composition of society, natural selection pressures still exist to ensure our environment is always changing. Even if that were not so, we would still continually evolve.

Historically haven't we always had a xenophobic fear of those that are different from us – something that no doubt helped us as cave dwellers when we only recognised our own particular tribe? But it seems we're still locking up those we see as eccentric or unconventional and medicating them to become deadened members of society. Isn't it time to recognise that these are some of the most valuable people in our society and ones that should be valued as such?

Didn't Richard Branson once suggest, with regard to business, that it's beneficial to employ someone left-field as they are the people who will come up with the next original idea? This seems to be what he meant when he said, 'Some of the best people we've ever hired didn't seem to fit in at first, but proved to be indispensable over time.' He credited these 'differences' with creating opportunities to see problems that others couldn't, as well as inspiring new creative energy. For instance, someone with Asperger's syndrome is likely to be the best person in a plane crisis, since they have the intense type of focused concentration that could coolly and unemotionally prevent a tragedy.

Women accept that men are more inclined to display characteristics on the Asperger's spectrum when they don't automatically notice that the rubbish needs to be taken out – and men in their turn complain that women are too concerned with emotional minutiae.

So how might we manage bipolar better in the community? Suggested options might include:

- Therapy: Learning about underlying issues associated with paranoid feelings to lessen their impact. For instance, rationalising inherent fears and how and why they might be tested or dealing with past relationships and how they may have impacted on current perspectives and how they could be dissolved or assimilated. Talking can be a way of bringing fears and paranoid feelings to the surface in a safe environment and ameliorating negative influences.

- Social support: Friends and family support for long-held fears of negative favouritism in the family or other issues that have been a distressing feature of their upbringing. When trust is lost, paranoia has the unfortunate side effect of eroding even the closest relationship if not kept under control.

- Support groups: These can be found through local community mental health centres, through doctors or other dedicated online bipolar help services like Bipolar UK, who are working to improve services for those suffering with the adverse effects of bipolar. Mind UK is a charity service that will add your name to a list for a counsellor who will offer limited weeks of therapy at a reduced fee according to your means. Rethink Mental Illness began in 1972 and works as part of the independent Mental Health Taskforce to improve lives by developing and establishing expert information, advice services and support groups for people severely affected by mental illness. They also provide training and launch local and national campaigns that have changed and continue to change how people and society as a whole view and behave towards people living with mental illness. The Mental Health Foundation maintains it is committed to working in partnership with other leading mental health organisations, professional bodies, academic institutions and fund organisations. They contend that they are a leading partner in most of the major mental health coalitions in the UK but their work and influence also extends internationally.

- Analytical therapy: A list of practising therapists can be found on The Analytic Network online. They claim that they are all fully qualified members of their professional associations and are registered by the UK Council for Psychotherapy, the British Psychoanalytic Council or equivalent and abide by the codes of ethics and practice of their member organisation and registering bodies. While they give details of how to contact them, they do not give any information about their fees and if you are to see them three or four times a week as recommended, you are going to need to be in a job that not only pays well but will allow you significant time off in order to attend your sessions.

- Cognitive analytic therapy (CAT): This seems to be the go-to therapy currently, and I have heard it described as 'revolving door therapy', meaning you just keep going around and around with little in the way of results. It is a therapy that aims to give a 'quick fix' by understanding why a person feels, thinks and behaves the way that they do before helping them problem-solve and develop new ways of coping. Of course, it helps some people to let go of their habitual ways of coping with stressful situations in a negative way, like PTSD, but while inherent problems take a lifetime to build up, solving them cannot be expected to work overnight.

It takes time for the psyche to let go of its long-held congenital beliefs and ways of processing information, and treatment for bipolar calls for a gentle and gradual approach, which, in my view is a time-consuming process if it's to have any long-lasting effect.

There are many other types of treatment out there and the National Institute for Health and Care Excellence (NICE) recommends the following types of talking therapies:

- Interpersonal therapy: Focusing on relationships with others. How thoughts, feelings and behaviour are affected by others.

- Behaviour couples therapy: Recognising and trying to resolve the emotional problems that can happen between partners.

- Family intervention: Talking therapy between the person experiencing mental health problems and their family members.

- EMDR (eye movement desensitisation and reprocessing): Being recommended by Prince Harry and Oprah Winfrey, which claims to reduce distressing emotions that particular memories and triggering situations bring on by systematic eye movement therapy.

If the way forward in managing mental 'illnesses' like bipolar is one of tolerance and understanding rather than seeking a 'cure', we will be required to rethink how we view these conditions. In the book *Madness Explained*, leading clinical psychologist Richard Bentall shatters the modern myths that surround psychosis. His work argues that we cannot define madness as an illness to be cured like any other, and that labels such as 'schizophrenia' and 'manic depression' are meaningless and based on nineteenth-century classifications. He argues that experiences such as delusions and hearing voices are, in fact, 'exaggerations of the mental foibles to which we are all vulnerable'.

It therefore appears likely that people in our modern society who suffer from mental disorders like bipolar are the casualties of archaic evolutionary development, but it also means that if we were to dispose of the gene that predisposes us to mental disorders, we would most likely also lose access to human creativity in the process – one of the most valuable parts of our genome.

So is it the creativity that makes people depressed or depression that makes people creative? Of course there is a stereotype linking creative people with mental conditions, depression in particular. But it's always possible that people involved in creative work are in themselves vulnerable people, and the more solitary and open-ended the activity they are involved in, the more vulnerable they are likely to be. It's also likely that people drawn to creative work are those who are naturally introspective and inward thinking. Perhaps genes contributing to mental problems have persisted across humanity in part because they also contribute to superior creativity. Shelley Carson, a Harvard psychologist and author of *Your Creative Brain*, says that although we are aware that mental disorders are not necessarily conducive to an individual, there may still be aspects of it that are beneficial overall to the human species.

If that is so, then I and many others like me might well be around for some time to come. After all, millions of our ancestors have proved themselves by passing the most rigorous quality controlled tests of natural selection, which allowed us to survive until today.

If we want to keep the most colourful and creative personalities in our society healthy, we need to appreciate and pay heed to the level of suffering that is part of these kinds of mental disorders, and provide what is needed, be it the right kind of medication, talking therapy or making sure they are in an environment where their levels of creativity and skills can be encouraged while keeping them balanced and preventing them from falling prey to their vicissitudes. With bipolar especially, we need to help sufferers develop the ability to maintain a reasonable balance without losing their creative output, but avoid some of the distress that swinging from one extreme mood to another can involve.

I was driving my grandson, Jake, home one Christmas from his father's, asking him more questions about his life, when the subject of bipolar came up. He turned to me and said, 'You must never let yourself get too high, Judy, or you will become equally as depressed at the other extreme.' He obviously was beginning to understand it while still only in his mid-teens.

Bentall, in his book, argues for a radical new way of thinking about psychiatric problems – one that does not reduce madness to brain chemistry but understands and accepts it as part of human nature. He makes an attempt to demystify psychosis and restore the patient to a proper place with the rest of humankind.

There is certainly some optimism for help in the future. A newsletter called 'Let's Talk Bipolar' was started in 1980 by Shelia Woodland in London. She originally placed an ad in *The Guardian* with a view to getting responses from people with the disorder.

Soon after, another ad was placed in the *The Times*, *The Daily Telegraph* and *The Observer* by Philomena Germing, and the two women got together and formed the society Bipolar UK in 1983. A number of common concerns were raised, namely:

-    GPs' and psychiatrists' evasiveness about the illness.

-    The conflicting advice offered by legal and medical professionals.

-    The major debate about whether manic depression is inherited or not.

In 2021 it would seem that few of these problems have been solved. For instance, the rate of suicide is a shocking three per day, and will most likely have increased during and after the pandemic of 2020–21, which will also have long-term results.

The society now runs eighty-five support groups around the country and since 1983 has focused on direct service provision to meet the needs of individuals affected by bipolar. In its newsletter, it says, 'As a small charity we have seen first-hand how dramatically demand for services has increased.'

It's also the society's aim to '…achieve parity or esteem for mental health services for people with bipolar'. It states that hundreds and thousands of people still lack basic support for this disorder and it is hoping to use digital technology to scale things up to ensure everyone with bipolar '…can live well and achieve their potential'.

On 20 March 2021 the Bipolar UK's Bipolar Commission launched its yearly enquiry to inform and improve the care and treatment of people living with bipolar. It estimates that two/three people diagnosed with bipolar die by suicide every day (seventy to ninety per cent of suicides are associated with manic-depressive illness or some other mood disorder being a contributory). It says the society wants to see a reduction in this number and better lives for people living with the disorder. It hopes to encourage more awareness and research to help achieve these goals.

The commission says that over the coming year they will be inviting people to submit evidence on different themes in two ways: through online surveys and independently through email. For this they will be asking people to complete an online survey about their individual experiences. Perhaps then we will understand the complexities of a condition that many sufferers, despite the unpredictability of their symptoms, would prefer to keep.

I would like to end with the findings of a new study, which has recently shed some more light on manic depression, asking 103 people who experience the disorder to decide whether they would wish to keep it because of the creative 'highs' it gives them or, alternatively, dispel it.

The survey, which was carried out by psychologists at Manchester University, discovered that twenty-six people decided they wanted to keep their disorder, feeling it was part of their personal identity, but seventy-seven did wish they could press a button to remove it.

It was felt that knowing there is such a difference in attitude towards bipolar disorder is helpful when selecting the best treatments. Some people obviously find that it is a part of their personality and would not wish to lose it completely, but would wish for a more personal type of clinical help to manage their more intense mood swings. The results were also felt to have an important impact on designing services for people with the diagnosis and perhaps working to help them with their low moods, leaving them their high creative ones.

The fact that it may be a biological predisposition in no way relieves society of its responsibility with regard to doing something about mental illness of this sort. With better, more compassionate treatments, people will feel less abject fear when facing these conditions than they do at the moment. The way counsellors and psychotherapist are trained to treat depression is frequently appalling. Genes are only part of the story, and treating what is called a biological imbalance with drugs is not the way forward. A hug or a walk in a sunlit forest or a stroll along a beach at sunset may be of far more benefit, as would someone to talk to who can understand you and change your perspectives to a more positive way of seeing the world and your place in it.

I will leave the last quote to another professional, someone who was a former psychiatrist and clinical director at the Bethlem Royal & Maudsley Hospital in London. In his tome, *The Master and his Emissary*, regarding the divided hemispheres of the brain, Iain McGilchrist asserts when commenting on bipolar disorder, that although some genes may have been expected to have impacted fertility because of their detrimental effect on the mental health of certain individuals, these genes would presumably have been bred out of the population long ago were it not for some huge benefit that eminated from them. Some cases have led to extraordinary talents being passed down despite the fact that bequeathed genes would have obviously been diluted, but would nevertheless have naturally been preserved according to purely Darwinian principles.

Just because certain people don't fit into the normal limited societal perimeters of conventionality, it doesn't mean they don't have a wealth of creative knowledge to offer society as well as an extraordinary and considerable range of unique gifts. So why should they be subject to abuse and ill treatment or be subdued and medicated – or even locked up with the inevitable loss of liberty as well as dignity – for their efforts to fit in?

Chapter 7

SELF-REALISATION

When my elder son Leon returned from Thailand after I'd booked to go and see him at Christmas, it was because his son Jake, my grandson, had been admitted to hospital in the Priory in Roehampton. It seemed another one of my immediate family was going to suffer from the disruptive disorder. Was it an inheritance that had been passed down yet again? It seemed so utterly unfair that an innocent young boy who had already had his fair share of physical issues, mainly from ecological problems, was now to be assailed with this capricious disorder. And he my only grandson, another highly intelligent and sensitive young boy, who I'd felt had an interesting future.

I had at last started to get down to writing my memoirs and, encouraged by my good friend Margot, whom I had met when she came to join my portrait classes, I'd enrolled myself into a writing club in nearby Frome, where I thought I might stay focused enough to finally get down to completing the project. I had been trying to make myself concentrate on writing my story since I had joined a writing class some eighteen years earlier. I was now approaching my octogenarian age; so if I didn't have enough material by now, I surely never would.

One morning in May 2019, on my way to my writing club, I got a frantic call from my son Leon to tell me that Jake was in hospital. His mother, who was now living in

Yorkshire, had been called to his bedside in the middle of the night and Leon needed to be there. I immediately offered to take him and found myself driving into London to pick him up and then driving at frantic speed up the M1 to Birmingham where Jake had been taken after he'd collapsed the night before after a party.

Although the doctors kept us in suspense until the next day, it was obvious to me that he would not recover sufficiently to be the same Jake I had so loved as a little boy; his infectious good humour had often had me in stitches, and his high intelligence was obvious to me even at an early age. But I knew he'd had problems with drugs during his twenty-five years and was potentially another family member with bipolar. While his father slept in a room beside him and the whole family stayed nearby overnight, the doctors decided the best course of action was to take him off his life support system the next day, and they declared he had died.

His father Leon was distraught. Although he'd gained a degree in computer studies when he'd got back from Thailand, he'd been unable to find or cope with any kind of steady employment. I found it impossible to take in the death of my only grandson, something that would bear out in the years to come as, at the time, I was more worried about the effect it would have on his father, Leon. And I was right to worry, as during the following Christmas my relationship with my elder son completely broke down. I greatly miss the extraordinary discussions I used to have with him each week, but with the effects of age, I was finding it hard to cope physically with all the distress.

The next year, 2020, I reached the grand old age of eighty, much to my astonishment. I was somewhat surprised I'd survived to tell the tale, let alone that I had not entirely lost my 'joie de vivre' – not even when the Covid pandemic lockdown hit the week of my birthday. I'd taken out a lifetime mortgage to make some improvements to my townhouse overlooking the Kennet and Avon canal and to purchase a hybrid car. On the day of my enforced isolated birthday celebration, I decided to put my newly acquired hybrid car through its paces and go somewhere I could take a long walk along a deserted beach on this first day of bright spring sunshine. I remembered one particular beach from my stay on the Gower peninsular, so I decided to drive to it along the M4. It was a long stretch of deserted beach and walking the length of it that beautiful spring day was well worth the long drive, even when a local gruffly informed me that only they were allowed on the beach. I arrived home at the end of the day to many congratulatory phone messages, as well as a huge bunch of beautiful flowers from Nicky lying on my doorstep.

Unfortunately, I picked up a speeding fine on the deserted motorway on my way home, but after I sent a letter of apology, the fine was later cancelled by the Welsh Pontypridd police (which I keep as trophy pinned to my wall-board). The mistake was said to be due to the lack of safe precautionary measures available at a time of Covid, something I had also pointed out. I didn't disclose that I had broken many of the speeding laws on my way there earlier, while driving along the long empty stretch of motorway.

In the summer I endured building problems when my conservatory was eventually built across the back of my house, having been held up for many months because of the Covid pandemic in 2020. Although the construction of it wasn't without its problems, it has turned out to be a very welcome addition to the house and somewhere I could sit in all weathers while swinging in my egg chair during the time of solitary lockdown measures enforced upon everyone during the pandemic. I even relished this great opportunity to get on with writing and not be diverted by other pursuits. Progress, perhaps, for someone with bipolar.

My life has been underlined with an unassailable desire to learn more about the psyche – my own as well as others' – and what makes us tick and what doesn't. It was for this reason that I stayed engaged in some sort of therapy until recently. I am still questioning how I came to be bipolar, as it is not organically in my family. Depression certainly comes down the line, but I believe it's only something I suffer from to rebalance the manic side of bipolar, allowing opposing forces to find some sort of equilibrium. Perhaps it has to be down to the timing of my birth during a world at war, the struggles with my mother's personality and my father's somewhat disturbing and austere behaviour.

With further thoughts on the subject of depression, psychoanalyst Donald Winnicott, in his book *Home is Where We Start From,* says that 'new experiences necessitate internal reassessment, and it is this reassessment we see as depression.' In other words, for us to move forward in our development, a period of sustained solitude is necessary to allow us to reassess our lives and stay mentally healthy. Perhaps the word depression would create less fear if we changed the name to 'introspection'. In the East, a mystic would think nothing of travelling into his unconscious on a daily basis – for them it is a healthy and beneficial way to behave – while for those in the West it's a fearful place and we refer to it disparagingly as depression whenever we encounter it.

While self-examination can be a painful process, emerging from a 'depression' can make me more self-aware and empathetic to others, even allowing me to feel I'm making some small progress to another level, while I admit a manic state produces the opposite effect. Of course, I'm not in either extreme state constantly; only certain emotional stresses affect me, and after a lifetime of trying to find beneficial ways of dealing with it, most people, I'm sure, would find it difficult to notice any difference in my behaviour.

Over the length of my lifetime I feel I've learned, at least to some extent, how to deal with this disruptive disorder called bipolar, which seems to be determined to affect some of the intellectually gifted and over-talented members of my family. It still means I have to pace myself, to make sure I get enough sleep, eat sensibly and try to avoid getting over-stimulated, on a daily basis. My management of the condition could also be down to the extensive therapy I've sought throughout my life, which has taught me so much more about conscious awareness. Perhaps there is also some advantage to being female, as our emotional templates aren't turned down so far as they are in men, allowing a woman to make more use of her right brain's emotional responses more readily, and therefore have a better chance of achieving a greater control of them.

It is still necessary to monitor my stress levels, as well as to prevent myself from going off on the euphoric flights of fancy that so excited me when I was young. With age, not only would they prove too exhausting, but they would inevitably lead to an equivalent depression in order to counterbalance the extreme. Naturally, your memory of the manic but euphoric experiences of old are retained; nevertheless while I feel it is inadvisable as well as unnecessary for me to keep repeating such overwhelming experiences, nor would I wish to erase them from my memory.

Having said that, when I recently told someone I felt it unlikely I'd have another grandchild after losing Jake, she responded, 'It would be a shame if there was never going to be anyone like you again.' I couldn't help replying, 'I certainly wouldn't want anyone else to have to face many of the dramas I've been through.'

So would I press the button to dispose of my bipolar disorder simply because of the dangerous depressions that go hand in hand with it? Probably not, because I feel I have lived more, loved more and found myself granted access to a far greater range of experiences and iconic journeys than I could have ever envisioned, due to its breath-taking intensity. I've found centres of creativity I could never have imagined discovering without it. I've moved more swiftly than I could have perceived towards understanding the limitless depths of emotions and the vulnerability of human nature, and how we attempt to consciously live and cope with the enormity of suffering and joy we encounter on the fitful odyssey that makes up our existence on this earth.

References

Chapter 2: What causes bipolar?

1) Carl Jung: Analytical Psychiatrist.
2) Professor Edward Bullmore: Psychiatrist and author. *The Inflamed Mind.*
3) Doctor Dorothy Rowe: Australian clinical psychologist. *The Successful Self.*
4) David Wigoder: Author. *Images of Destruction*
5) Donald Winnicott: Psychoanalyst. And author. *Home is Where We Start From.*
6) Giulia Enders: German scientist and author. *Gut*
7) Richard Bentall: Psychologist and author. *Madenss Explained.*
8) Robert Ploman: President of the International Behaviour Genetics Association and author. *Blueprint.*
9) Olav B. Smeland: Norwegian Centre for Mental Disorders (NORMAD).
10) Professor Catherine Gale, G.David Batty, Finn Rasmussen: University of Southampton.
11) Professor Daniel Smith: University of Glasgow, *The Guardian.*
12) Emil Kraeplin: Clinical Psychiatrist, Germany.

Chapter 3: What does bipolar feel like?

13) Hippocrates: Greek philosopher.
14) Prof. Kay Redfield Jamieson: Professor of Psychiatry at Johns Hopkins, USA and author *The Unquiet Mind* and *Touched with Fire.*
15) Adrian James: President of the NHS Royal College of Psychiatrists and Mind.

16) Anthony Storr: Psychiatrist and Author. *The Sanity of True Genius.*
17) Sylvia Plath: Author and poet.
18) R.D. Laing: Psychiatrist and author. *The Divided Self.*

Chapter 4: Bipolar and creativity

19) Theodora Lau, Author of *The Handbook of Chinese Horoscopes.*
20) Graham Greene. Author.
21) Neale Donald Walsch. Author of *Conversations with God.*
22) Arnold Ludwig. Author of *The Price of Greatness.*
23) Plato. Greek philosopher.
24) Edgar Allen Poe. Poet.
25) John W Robertson. Psychiatric study on Poe.
26) Alain de Botton. Philosopher and author of *Art as Therapy.*
27) Gordon Lord Byron. Poet.
28) Ada Lovelace. Writer, mathematician and computer pioneer.
29) Samuel Taylor Coleridge. Poet.
30) Sara Coleridge. Author and translator.
31) Bradford Keyes Mudge. Biographer.
32) Vincent van Gogh. Artist.
33) John Keats. Poet.
34) T.S. Eliot. Essayist.. Poet.
35) Virginia Woolf. Poet and author.
36) Robert Pinsky. Poet.
37) Jackson Pollock. Artist.
38) Stephen Fry. Author. TV Personality. Actor.
39) Tony Slattery. Actor.
40) Robin Williams. Screen actor.
41) Maria Carey. Singer and songwriter.
42) Carrie Fisher. Author. Screen actor.
43) Sandy Doyle. Journalist. Quartz Business Media magazine.
44) Mel Gibson. Screen actor.
45) Dr Douglas Bey Jr. Psychiatrist and author of *Loving a Depressed Man.*

46) Vivien Leigh. Actor.
47) Amy Winehouse. Singer and songwriter.
48) Dr David Sack. Addiction Treatment Centre, LA.
49) Catherine Zeta Jones. Actor.
50) Marjorie Wallace, CBE. Founder of mental health charity *Sane.*
51) Ruby Wax, OBE. Actor. Mindfulness expert. Author of *A Mindfulness Guide for the Frazzled.*
52) Kim Novak. Screen actor.
53) Dame Rachel Whiteread. Sculptor.
54) Dr Anthony Storr. Psychiatrist. Author of *The Sanity of the Genius.*
55) Marcel Proust. Author. Essayist.
56) Seneca. Roman philosopher.
57) John Dryden. Poet and critic.
58) Joe Griffin and Ivan Tyrrell. Authors of *Godhead.* Co-founders of Human Givens.

Chapter 5: Diagnosing and treating bipolar

59) Dr Lewis L. Judd. Psychiatrist.
60) Hospitalisation. *A Textbook on Psychiatry.*
61) Dr Arthur Christopoulos. Monash University. Australia.

Chapter 6: Cure of Manage?

62) The Observer. *Doctors fear new child mental health crisis.*
63) The Guardian. *Mental Health Issues.*
64) Tiffany Greenwood. Assoc. Prof. University of San Diago, US.
65) David Engleman. Neuroscientist. Author.
66) Prof. Jennifer Doudna. Biochemist. Nobel prize for CRISPR research.
67) Fredrich Nietzsche. Philosopher.

68) Jonathan Freedland. Journalist. Radio presenter.
69) Oswald Bumke. Psychiatrist. University of Munich.
     Author of *Handbook of Mental Diseases.*
70) Suzanne Hudson. Chief Exec. *Bipolar UK* (online mental
     health helpline)
71) Dr Benjamin Dean Hunt. Clinical trial coordinator.
72) Sir Richard Branson. Business magnate. Author.
73) Shelly Carson. Psychologist. Author of *Your Creative
     Brain.*
74) Iain McGilchrist. Author of *The Master and his
     Emissary.* Former psychiatrist and clinical   director of
     Bethlem and Maudsley Hospital.

www.ingramcontent.com/pod-product-compliance
Lightning Source LLC
Chambersburg PA
CBHW071215240726
48654CB00009B/787